DATE DUE

Better Homes and Gardens®

A Festive Christmas

BETTER HOMES AND GARDENS® BOOKS

Des Moines

BETTER HOMES AND GARDENS® BOOKS
An Imprint of Meredith® Books

A FESTIVE CHRISTMAS
Writer/Editor: Sylvia Miller
Designer: Angie Haupert Hoogensen, Mauck+Associates
Electronic Production Coordinator: Paula Forest
Production Manager: Douglas Johnston

Vice President and Editorial Director: Elizabeth P. Rice
Executive Editor: Kay M. Sanders
Art Director: Ernest Shelton
Managing Editor: Christopher Cavanaugh
Test Kitchen Director: Sharon Stilwell

President, Book Group: Joseph J. Ward
Vice President, Retail Marketing: Jamie L. Martin
Vice President, Direct Marketing: Timothy Jarrell

On the cover: Buttermilk Chocolate Cake, page 94

Meredith Corporation
Chairman of the Executive Committee: E.T. Meredith III
Chairman of the Board and Chief Executive Officer: Jack D. Rehm
President and Chief Operating Officer: William T. Kerr

All of us at Better Homes and Gardens Books are dedicated to providing you with the information and ideas you need to create delicious food. We welcome your questions, comments, or suggestions. Please write to us at: Better Homes and Gardens Books, Cookbook Editorial Department, RW 240, 1716 Locust Street, Des Moines, IA 50309-3023.

Our seal assures you that every recipe in *A Festive Christmas* has been tested in the Better Homes and Gardens Test Kitchen. This means that each recipe is practical and reliable, and meets our highest standards of taste appeal. We guarantee your satisfaction with this book for as long as you own it.

If you would like to order additional copies of any of our books, call 1-800-678-2803 or check with your local bookstore.

The Gift

It's not the dollars spent,

nor the hours and hours of work.

A Festive Christmas

is enjoying friends and family.

It is simple pleasures:

decorating the table with personal treasures,

sharing a meal with best friends,

reminiscing over coffee,

a Saturday spent making candy and cookies.

A Festive Christmas

is the aroma of fresh bread,

the flickering light of candles,

laughter around the punch bowl,

secrets and surprises.

Sharing a special recipe is a Christmas gift.

We hope you enjoy this book

as a gift that keeps on giving,

and we wish you A Festive Christmas,

year after year.

—THE EDITORS

Table of Contents

MARVELOUS MENUS

Your guests will eat, drink
and be merry as they enjoy
your delicious food and
beverages. (Turn to page 78 to
review the duck and game hen
dinners shown at right.) More
than 100 recipes in this
section provide the menu choices
to make you merry.

*Cookies, candies, and breads,
plus sauces, relishes and more
products of your kitchen,
convey the spirit of Christmas.
(See page 104 for cookies
shown here.) Enjoy both the
making and the giving of these
favorite things.*

Among My Favorite Things 98

*Cookies, candies, and breads are a part of family heritage
at Christmastime. Refresh the traditions with some new recipes.*

'Tis the Season

*Holiday entertaining time comes from
the calendar, and from the heart. 'Tis a warm,
festive feeling you want to share.
Serving food and beverages to friends and family is
a season tradition. It's not only what you serve,
but how you serve it that sets your party
apart from the others.
Candlelight is nearly magical. In this chapter,
you will see innovative ideas for using candles—
from arranging many on a glass cake stand
to fitting one inside an orange. Call guests to your
punch bowl with twinkling Christmas tree lights.
From the most elegant dinner to a very
relaxed and casual brunch, the table is the
centerpiece of holiday events. Dress your table for
guests with crystal and lace as well as napkin rings
made from tiny jingle bells. Like the prettiest
package under the tree, your presentation of food
shows that a little extra effort adds appeal.
'Tis the season to show your style.*

Deck The Table

*Th*e dining table is often the centerpiece of this jolly season. Your Christmas table creates a festive air when you apply a little attention and imagination to the setting.

Candleglow

Light your tables with the warm glow of flickering candles.

Arrange a variety of crystal candleholders in the center of a cake stand. Then, circle the plate with votives.

Add a festive touch to plain pillar candles. Acrylic paint and shiny dimensional paint make it easy. The holly-leaf design is just two wavelike strokes. Use dimensional paint for the berry dots.

Imagination

Get that glowing feeling with unique candlelight presentations. Any of these would be at home grouped among your dishes for a buffet supper.

Oranges add their tangy fragrance when they serve as tiny candle holders. Cut a slice off the top of each orange. (Cut a slice off the bottom, too, if necessary for balance.) Scoop out the pulp with a serrated grapefruit spoon. Press votive candles inside the oranges.

Walnut-shell candles float in a shallow bowl like a fleet of little ships. Melt white wax or pieces of white candles. Set walnut shells without cracks into egg cartons (to hold them steady). Pour melted wax into shells. Allow the wax to cool and partially harden before standing a birthday candle in each shell. When completely cool they are ready to set sail.

Canning jars create nostalgic luminarias. Place sand in the bottom of each jar and insert a candle. Vary jar styles and create a grouping for the best effect.

Twinkle

Christmas tree lights reflect
the sparkle in punch.
To make a punch bowl
wreath, twist 4- to 6-foot
grapevines or willow branches
together, forming a circle large
enough to fit around your
punch bowl. With wire, tie
vines together loosely at four
evenly spaced intervals. Let
stand several weeks till dry.
Remove wire; weave in or trim
loose ends. Spray with white
paint. Weave small, clear
Christmas tree lights through
branches. (Recipe for the
Quick Champagne Punch is
on page 56.)

Tie one on! Ribbon bows,
sprigs of greenery, cinnamon
sticks, and orange-peel stars
add festive flair. (Recipe for
Holiday Apple Fling
is on page 53.)

Decorated serving pieces put the
spotlight on the refreshments. Make your party food
the centerpiece of your table or buffet with the
addition of some festive trimmings.

*Texture variety adds appeal to both your
menu and your table setting. The red glass birds, red organdy
ribbon, and red roses provide three special surfaces
in one dramatic color.*

Red!

Crystal cardinals, red roses, and shimmery organdy ribbon are elements of classic elegance.
Use the organdy ribbon to tie sprigs of evergreen and a rose to your napkins.
Tuck a bird nest (filled with golden eggs) into a centerpiece of red roses and evergreen.

Willow branches complement the glass birds. Use an oversize willow-branch nest to hold your flowers.

Package tiny take-home gifts in fresh gaylax leaves. Simply wrap the top and bottom of the box separately and use a hot-glue gun to secure the leaves to the box. Festoon with an oversize red organdy ribbon bow.

Naturals meet craftsmanship in a folk-art setting.
Wood and fabric ornaments, baskets, pinecones, and painted
designs in simple motifs all work together to deliver
the Christmas spirit.

Folk Art Fun

A comfy country table is a wonderful setting for your tree-trimming party or any holiday get-together.
Tie ribbons on pinecones. Use velvety napkins for their softness. Scatter folk art Santas and ornaments over a colorful woven throw used as a tablecloth.

A sprig of cedar and a handmade button-covered tree ornament are tied to the neck of the dinner wine bottle.

Kids of any age will enjoy tree-covered glassware and matching napkins. All it takes is fabric or acrylic paint and an inexpensive paintbrush to apply the simple design.

Keeping to the gold, white, and crystal theme
of this setting gives you the opportunity to combine
heritage pieces with the most contemporary.
Set some new traditions.

Crystal and Gold

It glitters! And this extraordinary look is easy to achieve. Build on some treasured classics and add pieces keeping to the white, glass, and gold theme. Mirrors and simple crystal vases are tied together with gauzy gold ribbon. Crystal tree ornaments at each place setting convey the message that each guest is special.

A gilded mirror spotlights a sophisticated napkin tied with a charm-filled book mark. A Battenberg doily, adorned with crafts-store baubles, serves as a cover for a festive holiday beverage.

Cut flowers are tied with a ribbon to the outside of a vase that is filled with glass-and-gold ornaments.

Fruitful Efforts

Gilding is as elegant as you can get. Simply brush on a layer of thinned honey where you wish to apply gold leaf on firm, unblemished fruit. Gently place small pieces of gold leaf on the honey. You can find edible gold leaf (if it's 23 karats or more, it's edible) in well-supplied arts and crafts stores, as well as specialty food stores. A spray-on edible gold coating is also available. Gilding is a glorious way to glamorize your holiday table. The secret to success is working on a smooth surface. Simple ornaments and molded plastic fruit are two examples of items that gold transforms beautifully.

❖

It's also easy to sugar fruit. Add a tablespoon of water to three egg whites and beat until frothy. Use a small paintbrush or pastry brush to paint fruit (grapes, plums, etc.) with the egg white mixture, then sprinkle with sugar.

Add Christmas magic with fancy embellishments for everyday pears and oranges.

❖

Fragrant

Pomanders are a wonderful addition to your buffet. Display them with greens and wood shavings in a basket. To make pomanders, pierce the skin of an orange with a heavy needle and insert cloves in ornamental patterns.

Jingle
All the Way

*A jingle-bell napkin ring can
be a take-home treat for your
guests. String tiny jingle bells
on fine wire and shape into a
3-inch wreath. To make it do
dual duty as a place card,
thread a gift tag with the
guest's name among the bells.*

Everyone loves candy canes.
Tie silverware and a pair of
canes with a Christmas bow.
A bright plaid tablecloth
makes the perfect backdrop.
Find a warm, rich plaid at
your fabric store and enjoy it
on your table all winter.

*Festive additions to your table need not be
expensive or ostentatious. Think of Christmas motifs
that say merry and jolly.*

Personal

Present linens and china pieces
that you love to your guests.
Unmatched napkins,
placemats, cups, or dessert
plates come together when they
reflect your personality.

Treasures seldom come in matched sets of four, six, or eight. It doesn't matter. Unmatched collectibles can be combined in a table setting of unmatched grace.

Lace-edged linens and big doilies used as placemats look like snowflakes against a dark wood table.

Don't worry if you don't have matching napkins; fan-fold assorted crisp napkins and tie each with a bow.

Danish Christmas plates, lovingly collected through the years, usually hang on the wall or stay inside the china cabinet. Bring them to the table for salad or dessert plates to define your special holiday meal.

Give new meaning to your holiday table.
Let it be a showcase of keepsake linens. Bring collections out of the china cupboard for a charming setting that includes the family stories inherited with each treasure.

Homespun Tree

Build a tiny tree for your table or buffet from boxwood branches. Dried fruits, berries, and bows dangle from the boughs.

1

A Tree Grows

Begin with a large block of florists' foam. (See photo 1.) With a sharp knife, cut foam into the pyramid shape of a tree. Place the moistened tree form in a plastic saucer so the form fits snugly.

Poke boxwood branches into the foam (See photo 2.) Start at the bottom with longer pieces, flaring them downward to conceal the saucer. Taper your way up to the top with shorter pieces.

Decorate your tree, using a glue gun to affix apple rings, pieces of birch bark, pepper berries, pomegranates, cinnamon sticks, moss, and paper bows. (See photo 3.) Add a grapevine garland and top with a snowman.

Festive Decorating Ideas

An Alphabetical Starting Place for Imaginative Table Settings

APPLES — The rich red (and green, too) of apples shines when combined with holiday greenery. Apples also can be used as candle holders.

BAUBLES — Reserve bells, balls, and baubles from the tree to decorate your table. Paint names on balls (or write name in glue and dust with glitter) to use as place cards.

CANDLES — Use them profusely, in multiples!

COOKIES — Stand a Christmas cookie in front of each plate. Using a graham cracker as a platform, pipe frosting to hold your cookie upright. A little bag or jar of cookies at each place setting can be a take-home gift or dessert.

DINNERWARE — Christmas is a great time to mix it up. Use those collector Christmas plates for appetizers or bread.

EVERGREEN — Think about it in little snips and pieces. Tie a sprig with a napkin, tuck it among fruits in a basket or bowl.

FAMILY — Celebrate Christmases past by bringing out the family snapshots. Make simple painted cardboard "frames" and use them as place cards for the family dinner.

FLOWERS — Fresh bouquets, dried blossoms, and silk flowers add that special touch. Non-traditional Christmas blooms, when combined with evergreen, will take on a holiday air.

GINGERBREAD — Too many kitchen projects? Cut gingerbread men out of cardboard and paint them brown. Add white paint trim, glue on a little fabric heart.

HEIRLOOMS — Honor your heritage and use family keepsakes. Great-grandma's teapot could be your table centerpiece.

ICE — Freeze ice rings (or giant cubes made in muffin tins) to keep the punch bowl inviting. Decorate your ice with orange-peel stars *(see page 31)*.

JEWELRY — The costume jewelry you never wear is loaded with beads and baubles which can decorate a tiny tree, add glamour to a ribbon tied around napkins, or be pushed into a candle with straight pins.

KITCHEN — The delicious aromas drifting from the kitchen create a holiday atmosphere. When you aren't baking, simmer some spices in a saucepan.

LIGHT — Sink candles in coarse salt (it looks like snow) in a bowl.

MARBLES — In a vase or sprinkled on the table, glass marbles add a shiny touch.

MIRRORS — Use one under your centerpiece to reflect the colors and/or the candleglow. Use little framed mirrors under candleholders or ornaments.

MUSIC — Don't forget to add soft-playing Christmas music when you entertain.

NAPKINS — They don't need to match when you present them the same way. A big ribbon bow, a jingle bell ring, or tied with yarn and greenery, your assorted napkins will look great.

ORANGES — Make pomanders *(see page 21)* and tuck these fragrant oranges among greenery for your table centerpiece. Add orange candleholders *(see page 10)*.

PEARS — You don't need a partridge to decorate with pears. Gild fresh pears or plastic ones. *(See page 20 for ideas.)*

PINECONES — Make a gold-painted pinecone topiary *(photo, left)*. Decorate a pot (a gilding kit makes it easy). Put a plastic foam ball in the pot. Cut a stick to desired length, sharpen one end. Push pointed end into the foam ball, then hot-glue a gold-painted pinecone atop the stick. Cover the ball in the pot with moss and small pinecones.

QUILT — Use a quilt for a tablecloth and sprinkle it with crocheted doilies for a nostalgic holiday table backdrop.

RIBBON — Everything's better with bows. Choose wire-edged fancy ribbons or cut strips of fabric for your ties. Use the ribbons to carry your color scheme.

STARS — Irregular, long-pointed stars will make your table shine. Cut them from fabric and fuse them on a tablecloth and napkins. Cut them from foil wrapping paper and sprinkle them about. Cut them from wood and make candleholders.

TREES — Oh, Christmas tree, it can be ever so tiny. Form one from greenery for your buffet. Spray tiny twigs white and stick them in gumdrops for individual place-setting trees.

UPHOLSTER — Tie fabric slip-on covers over the backs of your chairs for a grand dinner. Dress up folding chairs this way.

VEGETABLES — Let a veggie be your bowl; present a dip or spread in a green, yellow, or sweet red pepper, seeded squash, or hollowed-out cabbage. Use a potato to stamp a simple Christmas motif on plain paper napkins. Cut your design into a potato and dip in acrylic paint to stamp in special effects. *(See photo, above.)* This is a great project for kids of any age.

WINE — Adorn your wine bottle with a bow and a sprig of greenery and/or trinkets tied about its neck.

WOOL — Warm, comforting woolen scarves and mittens are favorite things at Christmastime. Capture the feeling with strips of wool to tie your napkins, use as a tablerunner, or to fashion a snowman's scarf.

XEROX — Your convenient print shop can photocopy a Christmas motif or snapshots for you in multiples (and they can increase or reduce the size of the image). Use the copies to make place cards or invitations. Also look into the medium you can find at arts and crafts shops which transfers photocopies to fabric.

YARN — Like wool, yarn gives that warm, fuzzy feeling. Carry a color theme with tiny yarn bows on a miniature tree, tied around your stemware or napkins. Use the same color yarn to string beads.

ZIG-ZAG — You don't need to be an artist to create wonderful folk-art table linens. An uneven zig-zag border will brighten a placemat.

Fa La La Foods

*D*ressed for a party, the food deserves a few fancy fixings. It's the thought that counts when you add simple garnishes. When decorating a plate of appetizers or presenting dinner plates, use garnishes that repeat an ingredient to give guests a flavor clue.

Orange-Peel Stars

A simple punch becomes festive with floating garnishes. This Holiday Punch is a quick treat for a family engrossed in decorating the tree. Thaw two 12-ounce cans of frozen cranberry-raspberry juice cocktail concentrate and mix in two 1-liter bottles of orange-flavor carbonated water.

Garnish the punch bowl with spiced-apple rings and orange-peel stars. To make the floating stars, cut oranges in quarters, remove the pulp and flatten each rind section. Then press a small star-shape cutter through the peel.

Citrus Art

Oranges, lemons, and limes
provide a fresh look when used
to garnish foods. And these
citrus trims last well.

PRETTY PAIR

*Stack a slice of lemon on a
slice of lime, slash from the
center to the outside, then twist
in opposite directions for a
two-tone citrus twist.*

GIFT TIES

*Tie lemon or lime wedges with
a chive or narrow strip of
green onion.*

BLOOMING

*Using a thin, sharp knife,
thinly slice an orange in a
long, continuous strip of peel.
Coil the strip to form a rose.
Add tiny sticks of
lemon peel.*

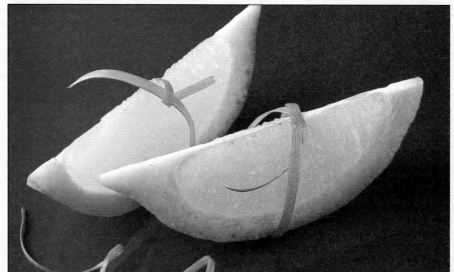

*Cut long, narrow strips of
citrus peel and have fun tying
knots. Combine orange, lime,
and lemon peels for
color appeal.*

GROOVY

*For notched slices, cut vertical
strips from a whole fruit with
a lemon zester, then slice.*

DEMURE

*A single lemon slice takes on
added interest when you slash
it from center to outside and
overlap the edges. Put a dab of
mayonnaise and an herb
leaf in the center.*

Fancy Flowers

A tomato rose nestles on a bed of greens on a platter of appetizers; cool cucumber flowers dress up seafood appetizers.

To make a tomato rose, cut a base from the stem end of a tomato, but do not sever the peel. Using a sharp, fine-bladed knife, continue peeling the tomato in a continuous narrow strip, tapering the end to remove the peel. Place the peel, flesh-side-up, on the cutting board. Beginning at the end opposite the base, roll the strip to form a rose shape.

The cucumber flower is made from thin crosswise slices of cucumber. Tightly roll up slices into a flower shape, overlapping slices to form petals. Secure with toothpicks and soak in salted ice water. Drain before using.

Herb Bouquets

Serving plates are made special with a tiny bouquet of herbs. (See photo, lower left.)

Select three or four different herbs with contrasting textures and colors, including a flowering herb, if possible. Cut stems to desired length (about 4 inches), arrange, and then tie the stems with string. The string used here was dyed with tea.

Herb bouquets can be made several hours or up to a day ahead. Place them flat on a damp paper towel in a storage container or plastic bag and store in the refrigerator.

Super Shapes

The shape makes a difference. For bread-based appetizers, cut bread into shapes with canapé cutters. If you don't have a set of cutters, substitute simple cookie cutters or cut square slices into diamonds and rectangles.

Piping quickly gives shape to a creamy, thick mixture. Try it with spreads such as deviled egg filling, cheese blends, or creamy chicken, seafood, or ham mixtures. Be sure to finely blend or chop all ingredients.

Eat, Drink, and Be Merry

*Fabulous foods and good fellowship are the
ultimate goals of holiday parties.
You may be hosting an open house for business
associates, the big family feast, an elegant
small dinner for best friends, a brunch or buffet
with out-of-town guests, or dessert and
coffee for neighbors. This section features beverages
and special coffees, all can be non-alcoholic or
spirited with equal good taste. Dishes for brunches
and buffets include many make-ahead
features to ensure that the event
is as relaxing for you as for your guests.
From game hens to a Christmas goose to a
traditional turkey dinner (shown, left), you'll find
extra dressings and sauces to make your bird
even better. Desserts include the mouthwatering
Buttermilk Chocolate Cake from the cover as
well as just-a-bite little sweets.
These recipes are selected for the holiday enjoyment
of both you and your guests.*

Open-House Appetizers

Planned parties or informal gatherings at your home become true holiday festivities when you serve trays of tempting appetizers. Enjoy sensational hosting with elegant foods while you simplify your life with make-ahead recipes.

1 package (10 ounces) frozen chopped spinach
1 package (8 ounces) cream cheese, softened
1/2 cup shredded cheddar cheese (2 ounces)
1 can (4 ounces) diced green chili peppers, drained
1/8 teaspoon garlic powder
1 can (6 1/8 ounces) skinless, boneless salmon, drained and flaked
8 flour tortillas (8-inch size)
1 container (8 ounces) soft-style cream cheese
1 to 2 tablespoons milk
  Fresh chives
1/4 cup finely snipped parsley

1. Cook spinach according to package directions. Drain thoroughly, squeezing out excess moisture. Finely chop spinach.
2. Meanwhile, beat the 8-ounce package cream cheese, cheddar cheese, chili peppers, and garlic powder with an electric mixer in a mixing bowl until combined. Divide cheese mixture in half. To one half of the mixture, stir in spinach. To remaining cheese mixture, stir in salmon.
3. To assemble, place one tortilla on a serving plate. Spread a generous *1/3 cup* spinach mixture on top. Place a second tortilla atop; spread with a generous *1/3 cup* salmon mixture. Repeat layers using five more tortillas and alternating spinach and salmon mixtures. Spread final layer with spinach mixture.
4. Place remaining tortilla on top. Combine soft-style cream cheese and enough milk to make of spreading consistency. Spread top and sides of torte with soft-style cream cheese mixture. Garnish top with fresh chives and snipped parsley; trim sides with remaining snipped parsley. Cover; chill for 4 to 24 hours.
5. To serve, carefully cut into narrow wedges using a very sharp knife.
Makes 24 servings.

Tortilla Sandwich Torte

PRESENTATION

The Tortilla Sandwich Torte (left) provides a decorated-cake look, but is an easy, make-ahead appetizer.

Greek-Style Cheese Ball

1 container (8 ounces) soft-style cream cheese
4 ounces dry-pack feta cheese
1/2 cup sliced ripe olives
3 tablespoons thinly sliced green onion
1 tablespoon snipped fresh basil *or* 1 teaspoon dried basil, crushed

1. Bring cream and feta cheeses to room temperature. Cut the feta cheese into chunks. In a blender container or food processor bowl combine cheeses. Cover and blend or process till smooth.
2. Reserve *1 tablespoon* of the olives and *1 tablespoon* of the onion. Chop remaining olives. Stir the chopped olives, remaining onion, and basil into cheese mixture. Shape into ball. Cover and chill till serving time.
3. Sprinkle cheese ball with reserved green onion and sliced ripe olives. Makes 24 (1-tablespoon) servings.

Crostini with Roasted-Pepper Spread

12 ounces baguette-style French bread
1/2 cup olive oil
2 tablespoons finely snipped fresh basil
1/2 teaspoon garlic powder
1/2 teaspoon lemon-pepper seasoning
1 small onion, finely chopped
1 tablespoon olive oil
1 jar (12 ounces) *or* 2 jars (7 1/4 ounces each) roasted red peppers, drained
1 can (7 1/2 ounces) tomatoes, cut up
1 teaspoon fennel seed, crushed
1/2 teaspoon sugar
1/4 teaspoon salt
1/4 teaspoon pepper

1. For crostini, cut French bread into 1/4-inch slices. Place slices in a single layer on baking sheets; set aside. Combine 1/2 cup olive oil, basil, garlic powder, and lemon pepper. Brush on one side of each slice of bread. Broil each sheet 3 to 4 inches from heat about 2 minutes till toasted. Turn bread slices over and broil 1 to 2 minutes more or till toasted. Repeat with remaining bread. Cool. Store in plastic bag.
2. Cook onion in the 1 tablespoon olive oil in a 10-inch skillet till tender but not brown. Add drained red peppers, *undrained* tomatoes, fennel, sugar, salt, and pepper. Bring to boiling; simmer, uncovered, for 10 minutes or till most of liquid is evaporated. Cool slightly. Transfer to blender container; process till smooth. Transfer to bowl. Cover and chill for up to 4 days.
3. Let stand at room temperature for 30 minutes before serving. Serve with toasted crostini. Makes 30 appetizer servings.

Fruit-Nut Snack Mix

4 cups bite-size twist pretzels
1 cup dried tart cherries
1 cup salted mixed nuts
1 cup banana chips

1. In a large bowl combine all ingredients. Store in an airtight container for up to 1 week. Makes 7 cups.

*The Fruit-Nut Snack Mix,
Greek-Style Cheese Ball and
Pimiento Butter can be made
ahead and kept waiting to
welcome drop-in guests.*

1   jar (4 ounces) pimiento pieces, drained
1   tablespoon anchovy paste
1   clove garlic, minced
1/2 cup margarine *or* butter, softened
    French bread

Pimiento Butter

1. In a blender container or food processor bowl combine pimientos, anchovy paste, and garlic. Cover and blend or process till smooth and pimientos are pureed. Stir mixture into margarine. Spoon into a serving dish. Cover; chill. To serve, let margarine mixture stand, covered, at room temperature for 30 minutes to soften. Serve with French bread. Makes about 1 cup.

1   cup packaged biscuit mix
1/2 cup shredded Monterey Jack cheese with jalapeno peppers (2 ounces)
2   tablespoons cornmeal
2   tablespoons chopped pimiento
1/3 cup beer

Chili-Cheese Bites

1. In a medium bowl stir together the biscuit mix, shredded cheese, cornmeal, and pimiento. Stir in beer. Let stand for 5 minutes.
2. Drop batter by teaspoons onto a greased baking sheet. Bake in a 450° oven for 7 to 10 minutes or till golden. Serve warm. Makes 24.

Cater to your guests with Herbed Pork Pâté and Spinach-Topped Polenta Bites (recipes, right).

Salami Egg Cups

6 hard-cooked eggs
1 ounce salami, finely chopped (¹/₃ cup)
2 tablespoons dairy sour cream
2 tablespoons mayonnaise *or* salad dressing
2 tablespoons snipped parsley
1 teaspoon Dijon-style mustard
  Parsley springs (optional)
2 cups shredded lettuce

1. Cut eggs in half crosswise; cut a thin slice from the end of each egg so egg halves set evenly. Remove yolks from eggs and place in a mixing bowl. Mash yolks with a fork till almost smooth. Stir in salami, sour cream, mayonnaise or salad dressing, snipped parsley, and mustard; mix well.
2. Spoon egg-yolk mixture into egg-white cups. Garnish each cup with a tiny parsley sprig, if desired. Cover and chill for 4 to 24 hours. To serve, arrange lettuce on serving plate and nestle egg cups in the lettuce. Makes 12 servings.

12 ounces ground pork
$^1/_2$ cup chopped onion
2 cloves garlic, minced
4 ounces beef liver, cut up, *or* chicken livers, halved
$^3/_4$ cup milk
2 eggs
2 tablespoons fine dry bread crumbs
1 tablespoon cornstarch
1 teaspoon dried basil, crushed
$^1/_2$ teaspoon dried rosemary *or* thyme, crushed
6 thin asparagus spears *or* thin carrot sticks (about $3^1/_2$ inches long), cooked
Assorted crackers and breads
Fresh herbs (optional)
Carrot curls (optional)

1. Grease bottom and sides of a $7^1/_2$ x $3^1/_2$ x 2-inch loaf pan. Line bottom with foil. Grease foil.
2. Cook pork, onion, and garlic in a large skillet till meat is just brown. Add liver; cook and stir over medium-high heat 3 to 4 minutes or till liver is no longer pink. Drain; cool slightly.
3. Place liver mixture and milk in a blender container or food processor bowl. Cover and blend or process till smooth. Add eggs, crumbs, cornstarch, herbs, $^1/_2$ teaspoon *salt,* and $^1/_4$ teaspoon *pepper.* Cover; blend thoroughly.
4. Pour *half* of mixture into prepared pan. Arrange asparagus or carrot sticks atop. Top with remaining mixture. Cover pan with foil. Place in larger baking pan in oven; pour 1 inch hot water into larger pan. Bake in 325° oven 1 to $1^1/_4$ hours or till knife inserted off center comes out clean and meat thermometer inserted in mixture registers 170°. Remove foil. Cool in pan. Cover; chill.
5. Serve with crackers and bread; garnish with herbs and carrot curls, if desired. Makes 15 to 20 servings.

1 cup cornmeal
$^1/_4$ cup grated Romano *or* Parmesan cheese
1 package (10 ounces) frozen chopped spinach, thawed and well drained
2 containers (4 ounces each) semisoft spiced garlic and herbs cheese
$^2/_3$ cup finely chopped toasted pine nuts *or* almonds
8 ounces (2 cups) shredded provolone *or* mozzarella cheese
Thin sweet pepper strips

1. Bring 3 cups *water* to boiling in medium saucepan. In mixing bowl combine cornmeal, 1 cup *cold water,* and 1 teaspoon *salt.* Slowly add cornmeal mixture to boiling water, stirring constantly. Cook and stir till mixture boils. Reduce heat to low; cook 10 to 15 minutes or till very thick, stirring occasionally. Stir in Romano or Parmesan. Turn into lightly greased 15x10x1-inch baking pan. Cool 1 hour. Chill just till firm.
2. Pat spinach dry with paper towel. In bowl stir together spinach, spiced cheese, pine nuts, and *1 cup* provolone.
3. Cut circles from the polenta, using a 2-inch-round cutter. Spoon spinach mixture atop the rounds. Place on a lightly greased baking sheet. Sprinkle with remaining provolone or mozzarella. Cover and chill up to 24 hours.
4. To serve, uncover and bake in a 350° oven for 10 to 12 minutes or till heated through. Garnish with thin strips of sweet pepper, if desired. Makes 32.

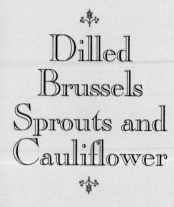

Dilled Brussels Sprouts and Cauliflower

2 cups brussels sprouts *or* one 10-ounce package frozen brussels sprouts
1 cup cauliflower flowerets
1/4 cup olive oil *or* salad oil
3 tablespoons vinegar
1 tablespoon lemon juice
1 teaspoon dried dillweed
1 jar (2 ounces) sliced pimiento, drained
Lettuce leaves (optional)

1. In a saucepan cook the fresh brussels sprouts and cauliflower in a small amount of boiling water for 8 to 10 minutes or till crisp-tender. (*Or,* cook frozen brussels sprouts according to package directions, *except* omit salt.) Drain. Halve any large pieces. Place in a medium mixing bowl.

2. In a small saucepan combine olive or salad oil, vinegar, lemon juice, and dillweed. Bring just to boiling. Pour over brussels sprouts and cauliflower. Cool. Cover and chill at least 2 hours, stirring occasionally.

3. To serve, add sliced pimiento to vegetable mixture; stir gently. If desired, line a small platter with lettuce leaves. Using a slotted spoon, transfer the vegetable mixture to the platter or to a serving bowl. Makes 10 to 12 servings.

Plum-Good Mini-Ribs

3 pounds pork loin back ribs, sawed in half across the bones
1/2 cup red plum jam
1/4 cup soy sauce
1/4 cup water
3 tablespoons vinegar
2 tablespoons cornstarch
1 clove garlic, minced
2 green onions, finely slivered
1/8 of a red onion, slivered

1. Cut ribs into single-rib portions. Rinse. Place ribs in a Dutch oven; cover with *water.* Cover pan and simmer about 45 minutes or till ribs are almost tender. Drain ribs and place, meaty side up, in a foil-lined shallow roasting pan.

2. Meanwhile, for sauce, combine jam, soy sauce, water, vinegar, cornstarch and garlic in a small saucepan. Cook and stir over medium heat till mixture is thickened and bubbly.

3. Brush ribs with plum sauce. Bake, uncovered, in a 350° oven for 15 minutes or till ribs are tender and well glazed.

4. Cool ribs. Place in a covered refrigerator container and refrigerate for 8 to 24 hours. Or, to freeze, arrange cooked ribs in a single layer in a freezer container or wrap in moisture- and vapor-proof wrap in a single layer. Seal, label, and freeze for up to 2 months.

5. To serve, place ribs in a single layer in a shallow baking pan; cover pan loosely with foil. Heat in a 350° oven about 45 minutes for frozen ribs and about 20 minutes for refrigerated ribs or till hot. Transfer ribs to serving platter; sprinkle with slivered green and red onions. Makes 12 servings.

1 can (15 ounces) garbanzo beans, drained
1/2 cup plain yogurt
1/4 cup buttermilk salad dressing
2 tablespoons fine dry seasoned bread crumbs
2 teaspoons lemon juice
1/2 teaspoon crushed red pepper
2 tablespoons chopped pitted ripe olives
   Chopped radishes (optional)
   Assorted vegetable dippers, such as baby carrots, zucchini slices, radishes,
      broccoli flowerets, red sweet pepper strips

1. Combine garbanzo beans, yogurt, salad dressing, bread crumbs, lemon juice, and red pepper in a food processor bowl or blender container. Cover and process or blend till mixture is smooth. Stir in olives. Transfer to a serving bowl. Chill, covered, at least 1 hour.
2. To serve, garnish with chopped radishes, if desired. Serve with vegetable dippers. Makes about 1 2/3 cups dip.

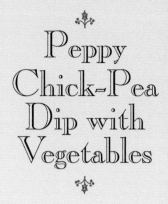

Peppy Chick-Pea Dip with Vegetables

DIP IN

Pep up popular vegetable dippers with a bowl of Peppy Chick-Pea Dip

Crab Mousse Morsels

36 slices party rye bread
 1 envelope unflavored gelatin
 1 teaspoon instant chicken bouillon granules
1/2 teaspoon sugar
2/3 cup mayonnaise or salad dressing
 2 tablespoons cocktail sauce
 1 tablespoon lemon juice
 1 tablespoon minced parsley
 1 can (6 ounces) crabmeat, drained, finely flaked, and cartilage removed
1/4 cup very finely chopped red sweet pepper
1/4 cup whipping cream, whipped
    Garnishes: Thin cucumber pieces, red pepper pieces, and/or snipped parsley

1. Cut shapes from bread with hors d'oeuvre cutters. Cover and set aside.
Combine gelatin, bouillon, sugar, and 1/2 cup *water* in small saucepan; let stand 5
minutes. Cook and stir till gelatin is dissolved. Remove from heat.
2. Combine the mayonnaise, cocktail sauce, lemon juice, and the 1 tablespoon parsley;
stir in gelatin mixture. Chill till partially set (like unbeaten egg whites).
3. Fold crabmeat, red pepper, and cream into gelatin mixture. Chill just till mixture
mounds. Spoon into pastry bag fitted with large star tip.
4. Pipe mousse onto each bread cutout. Garnish as desired. Cover carefully. Chill up to
4 hours. Makes 36.

*Crab Mousse Morsels and
Endive with Antipasto make
classy presentations
for your party.*

2 heads Belgian endive
1 jar (6 ounces) marinated artichokes, drained and chopped
1/2 cup chopped zucchini
2 ounces salami, chopped (1/3 cup)
1/4 cup chopped pitted ripe olives
3 tablespoons creamy garlic or green goddess salad dressing

1. Wash and separate endive leaves; pat dry. Chill in plastic bag. Combine artichokes, zucchini, salami, olives, and dressing. Cover and chill.
2. To serve, spoon artichoke mixture into endive leaves. Makes about 32.

1 1/2 pounds medium shrimp (about 36), peeled and deveined
36 fresh pea pods
2 tablespoons margarine or butter
4 teaspoons all-purpose flour
1/2 cup light cream or half-and-half
1/2 cup dairy sour cream
1/4 cup white wine vinegar
2 tablespoons Dijon-style mustard
1/4 teaspoon dry mustard
1 tablespoon capers, drained (optional)

1. Cook shrimp, uncovered, in boiling water 2 minutes or till pink. Drain.
2. Cook pea pods, covered, in small amount of lightly salted, boiling water 3 minutes or till tender. Drain, rinse, and cool. Wrap pods around shrimp. Secure with wooden picks. Cover; chill.
3. Melt margarine in small saucepan. Stir in flour. Add cream all at once. Cook and stir over medium heat till thickened. Cook and stir 1 minute more. Remove from heat. Stir in sour cream, vinegar, mustards, and 1/2 teaspoon *pepper*. Pour into serving bowl; cover and chill. Sprinkle with capers, if desired. Serve shrimp with sauce. Makes 36.

16 large fresh mushrooms (about 1 pound)
1 package (3 ounces) cream cheese, softened
3 tablespoons crumbled blue cheese
2 tablespoons chopped walnuts
1 tablespoon snipped chives or thinly sliced green onion
Lettuce

1. Remove stems from mushrooms and set aside for another use (in a soup or skillet meal, for example). Steam mushroom caps in a small amount of boiling *water* in a covered saucepan for 6 to 8 minutes. Drain and invert caps on paper towels; set aside to cool while preparing filling.
2. Beat the cream cheese and blue cheese together in a small bowl. Stir in nuts. Spoon mixture into mushroom caps and sprinkle with chives or green onion. To serve, arrange on a lettuce-lined plate. Makes 16.

Spirited Beverages

Toast the holidays with warm, chill-chasing drinks and sparkling partytime punch. The tradition of hot spiced drinks (mulled) comes from 17th-century England, where a poker was heated in the fireplace and plunged into a drink to warm it.

2   cups hot brewed coffee
    Chocolate-Dotted Cream
    Chocolate curls (optional)

1. Pour coffee into 4 cups. Pipe or spoon Chocolate-Dotted Cream over coffee in each. Top with chocolate curls, if desired Makes 4 (6-ounce) servings.
    Chocolate-Dotted Cream: In small mixer bowl, beat 1/2 cup whipping cream, 2 tablespoons sugar, and 1 teaspoon vanilla with an electric mixer on low speed till soft peaks form. Fold in 1 ounce German sweet chocolate, grated. Makes about 2 cups.

1/2   cup whipping cream
  1   tablespoon powdered sugar
  2   cups hot espresso coffee
      Freshly shredded orange peel

1. Beat together whipping cream and powdered sugar till stiff peaks form. Pour espresso into 6 small cups, filling cups half full. Add a large spoonful of whipped cream to each. Sprinkle with orange peel. Serve immediately or gently stir till whipped cream is melted. Makes 6 cups.
    Iced Cappuccino: Follow directions above, *except* use cooled brewed espresso. Pour over ice in glasses. Top with whipped cream and orange peel as above. Makes 6 servings.

Chocolate Café au Lait

Cappuccino

ELEGANT

Cappuccino in china cups or Iced Cappuccino in crystal stemware (photo, left) ends an evening with a fine flourish.

Café Alexander

¹/₂ cup hot coffee
1 tablespoon crème de cacao
1 tablespoon brandy
Whipping cream
Ground cinnamon or nutmeg

1. Pour coffee into a cup or mug. Stir in crème de cacao and brandy. Top with a dollop of whipped cream; sprinkle with cinnamon or nutmeg. Makes 1 (6-ounce) serving.

Café Caribe: Follow directions for Café Alexander, substituting 1 tablespoon *coffee liqueur* and 1 tablespoon *rum* for crème de cacao and brandy.

Café Dublin: Follow directions for Café Alexander, substituting 1 tablespoon *Irish whiskey* and 2 teaspoons *sugar* for crème de cacao and brandy.

Café Holland: Follow directions for Café Alexander, substituting 2 tablespoons *chocolate-mint liqueur* for crème de cacao and brandy.

Café Israel: Follow directions for Café Alexander, substituting 2 tablespoons *chocolate-flavored syrup* and 2 tablespoons *orange liqueur* for crème de cacao and brandy.

Café Noix: Follow directions for Café Alexander, substituting 2 tablespoons *amaretto* or *Fra Angelica* for crème de cacao and brandy.

Spiced Cranberry Tea

6 inches stick cinnamon, broken
2 teaspoons whole cloves
1 cup water
¹/₄ cup sugar
1 quart apple cider
3 cups strong tea
1 can (12 ounces) frozen cranberry-raspberry juice concentrate *or* cranberry juice cocktail concentrate
Lemon slices (optional)
Fruit-flavor striped candy sticks (optional)

1. Tie cinnamon and cloves in the center of a 6-inch square of 100-percent-cotton cheesecloth. Set spice bag aside.
2. Combine water and sugar in a 4-quart Dutch oven. Heat and stir till sugar dissolves. Add spice bag, cider, tea, and juice concentrate. Heat through. Discard spice bag. Pour into a heatproof punch bowl. If desired, add lemon slices. Ladle into mugs and serve hot with candy sticks for stirrers, if desired. Makes 16 to 18 (4-ounce) servings.

White Christmas Punch

3 quarts vanilla ice cream
2 cups bourbon
1 cup light rum
14 cups milk
Ice ring (optional)

1. In a large bowl stir the vanilla ice cream just till softened; blend in bourbon and rum. Cover and place in the freezer till needed.
2. At serving time, transfer ice cream mixture to a punch bowl. Blend in milk, stirring slowly with up-and-down motion. Float ice ring atop punch, if desired. Makes about 50 (4-ounce) servings.

1 can (6 ounces) *each* frozen cranberry juice cocktail concentrate, frozen orange juice concentrate, and frozen pineapple juice concentrate, thawed
1 bottle (750 milliliters) dry white wine
3 bottles (10 ounces each) carbonated water

Mix concentrates in a 3-quart pitcher; cover and chill. To serve, add wine and carbonated water; mix well. Serve over ice. Makes 16 (6-ounce) servings.

Fruit-Wine Punch

SWEET

Coffee Eggnog, served with your favorite cookies, invites guests to linger.

Coffee Eggnog

1 tablespoon hot water
1 1/2 teaspoons instant coffee crystals
4 cups eggnog
2 tablespoons brown sugar
1/8 teaspoon ground cinnamon
1/4 cup coffee liqueur (optional)
1/4 cup brandy *or* bourbon (optional)
1/2 cup whipping cream
1/4 cup sifted powdered sugar
1/2 teaspoon vanilla
Instant coffee crystals (optional)

1. In a large mixing bowl combine hot water and the 1 1/2 teaspoons coffee crystals; stir to dissolve. Add eggnog, brown sugar, and cinnamon. Beat with a rotary beater or whisk till sugar is dissolved. Stir in coffee liqueur and brandy or bourbon. Chill thoroughly.
2. At serving time, in a small mixer bowl beat whipping cream, powdered sugar, and vanilla with an electric mixer on high speed till soft peaks form. Pour eggnog mixture into 4-ounce cups or glasses; top with whipped cream and sprinkle with additional coffee crystals, if desired. Makes 8 to 10 (4-ounce) servings.

Creamy Eggnog

6 beaten eggs
2 cups milk
1/4 cup sugar
2 to 4 tablespoons light rum
2 to 4 tablespoons bourbon
1 teaspoon vanilla
1 cup whipping cream
Ground nutmeg

1. In a heavy medium saucepan combine eggs, milk, and sugar. Cook and stir over medium heat till mixture coats a metal spoon. Remove from heat; cool at once by placing pan in sink or bowl of ice water and stirring 1 to 2 minutes. Stir in rum, bourbon, and vanilla. Chill at least 6 hours or overnight.

2. At serving time, whip the cream. Transfer egg mixture to punch bowl; fold in whipped cream. Serve immediately. Top each serving with nutmeg. Makes 10 (4-ounce) servings.

Creamy Chocolate Eggnog: Prepare as directed above, except substitute 1/2 cup *chocolate-flavored syrup* for the rum and bourbon. Add 2 to 4 tablespoons *crème de cacao* and 2 to 4 tablespoons *amaretto*, if desired.

Irish Chocolate Milk

1 pint vanilla ice cream
1/4 cup Bailey's Irish Cream
2 tablespoons crème de cacao
3 tablespoons chocolate syrup

1. Combine vanilla ice cream, Irish Cream, and crème de cacao in a blender container. Blend till well mixed. Divide *half* the chocolate syrup among three wineglasses. Divide ice-cream mixture among glasses. Drizzle remaining chocolate syrup over mixture in glasses. Makes 3 servings.

Citrus Punch

1 medium seedless orange
1 lemon
1 lime
1/2 cup orange liqueur
1/2 cup brandy
3 tablespoons honey
1 bottle (750 milliliters) dry white wine, chilled
1 bottle (28 ounces) carbonated water, chilled

1. Thinly slice orange, lemon, and lime. In a bowl stir together liqueur, brandy, and honey. Add fruit slices. Cover and chill several hours.

2. At serving time, pour honey mixture into a punch bowl or pitcher. Stir in wine and carbonated water. Serve over ice. Makes 16 (4-ounce) servings.

See photo page 13.

Holiday Apple Fling

1 jar (14 ounces) spiced apple rings
1 bottle (32 ounces; 4 cups) cranberry-juice cocktail
1 bottle (32 ounces) apple juice
4 to 5 inches stick cinnamon
  Peel from 1 orange
1 bottle (750 milliliters) champagne *or* 1 bottle (28 ounces) ginger ale, chilled
  Cinnamon sticks (optional)
  Spiced apple rings (optional)
  Orange-peel stars (optional)

1. Drain apple rings, reserving syrup. In a 3-quart container combine reserved syrup, cranberry-juice cocktail, 2 cups of the apple juice, 1 cup water, and the stick cinnamon. Cover; chill for 24 hours. Remove cinnamon. Chill, covered, for up to 2 weeks.
2. In a 4-cup ring mold, freeze a little of the remaining apple juice just till slushy (about 30 to 45 minutes). Using an hors d'oeuvre cutter, cut orange peel into stars. Press stars into slushy apple juice in the mold. Center apple rings over stars. Freeze till firm. Add remaining apple juice to mold. Freeze for up to 2 weeks.
3. To serve, unmold ice ring; place in a large punch bowl. Add syrup mix. Slowly add champagne or ginger ale. Serve at once with cinnamon-stick stirrers, additional apple rings, and additional orange-peel stars, if desired. Makes about 24 (4-ounce) servings.

Pitcher of Gold

1 can (18 ounces) unsweetened pineapple juice, chilled
1 can (12 ounces) apricot nectar, chilled
1 can (6 ounces) frozen orange juice concentrate, thawed
2 cans (12 ounces each) lemon-lime carbonated beverage, chilled

Stir fruit juices together in a 2-quart pitcher. Add carbonated beverage, stirring gently to mix. Serve over ice. Makes 10 (6-ounce) servings.

Lemon-Apricot Slush

2 tablespoons instant tea powder
3 cans (12 ounces each; 4$^{1}/_{2}$ cups) apricot nectar
$^{1}/_{2}$ of a 6-ounce can ($^{1}/_{3}$ cup) frozen lemonade concentrate
1 bottle (10 ounces; 1$^{1}/_{4}$ cups) ginger ale
$^{3}/_{4}$ cup bourbon (optional)

1. Combine tea powder and 1 cup *water* in a large bowl; stir in nectar, concentrate, ginger ale, and bourbon, if desired. Pour mixture into a shallow freezer container. Cover, seal, label, and freeze.
2. To serve, let frozen mixture stand at room temperature for 30 to 45 minutes or till partially thawed; stir and spoon into glasses. If made without bourbon, stir additional ginger ale into each serving. Makes 12 (5-ounce) servings.

Hot Buttered Cider

The rich colors of Hot Buttered Cider, Hot Cranberry Toddy, Mulled Pineapple Punch, and Glogg are as inviting as the warm, spicy flavors.

7 cups apple cider *or* apple juice
1/3 cup packed brown sugar
4 inches stick cinnamon
1 teaspoon whole allspice
1 teaspoon whole cloves
　 Peel from 1 lemon, cut into strips
1 to 1 1/2 cups rum
　 Butter *or* margarine
　 Thin apple slices (optional)

1. Combine apple cider or apple juice and brown sugar in a large saucepan. For spice bag, tie cinnamon, allspice, cloves, and lemon peel in a 6-inch square of 100-percent-cotton cheesecloth. Add spice bag to cider mixture.

2. Bring cider mixture to boiling. Reduce heat and simmer, covered, for 15 minutes. Remove and discard spice bag. Stir in rum. Pour cider mixture into mugs. Float about 1/2 teaspoon butter or margarine on each. Top each serving with one or two thin apple slices, if desired. Makes about 10 (6-ounce) servings.

  6 cups cranberry juice cocktail
¹/₂ cup sugar
  3 strips (each 1 inch long) lemon peel
¹/₄ cup lemon juice
  3 inches stick cinnamon
  1 teaspoon whole cloves
¹/₃ cup bourbon, rum, *or* orange juice
    Lemon peel (optional)

1. Combine cranberry juice cocktail, sugar, lemon juice, and 2 cups *water* in a 4-quart saucepan or Dutch oven.
2. For spice bag, tie lemon peel, cinnamon, and cloves in a 6-inch square of 100-percent-cotton cheesecloth. Add spice bag to saucepan. Bring just to boiling; reduce heat. Simmer, covered, 10 minutes. Discard spice bag. Add bourbon, rum or orange juice.
3. Transfer to a heatproof serving carafe or pot. Serve with a lemon-peel strip in each cup, if desired. Makes about 12 (6-ounce) servings.

  3 cups unsweetened pineapple juice
  2 cups unsweetened white grape juice
  1 cup water
¹/₂ of a 6-ounce can frozen lemonade concentrate, thawed (¹/₃ cup)
¹/₄ cup packed brown sugar
  6 inches stick cinnamon, broken
  1 teaspoon whole cloves
  1 teaspoon whole allspice
    Whole cranberries (optional)

1. Combine pineapple juice, grape juice, water, lemonade concentrate, and brown sugar in a large saucepan. For spice bag, tie cinnamon, cloves, and all-spice in a 6-inch square of 100-percent-cotton cheesecloth; add to juice mixture. Bring to boiling. Reduce heat and simmer, covered, 10 minutes. Remove bag. Serve in heatproof glasses or cups. Garnish with cranberries on skewers, if desired. Makes about 8 (6-ounce) servings.

  1 bottle (750 milliliters) dry red wine
¹/₂ cup raisins
¹/₂ cup gin, vodka, *or* aquavit
¹/₃ cup sugar
    Peel from 1 orange
  8 inches stick cinnamon, broken
  6 whole cloves
  2 cardamom pods, opened
¹/₄ cup blanched whole almonds

1. Stir together wine; raisins; gin, vodka, or aquavit; and sugar in a large saucepan. For spice bag, tie orange peel, cinnamon, cloves, and cardamom in a 6-inch square of 100-percent-cotton cheesecloth. Add to wine mixture.
2. Heat mixture to simmering. Simmer, uncovered, for 10 minutes. Do not boil. Remove and discard the spice bag. Stir in almonds just before serving. Makes 8 (4-ounce) servings.

Party Punch Base

1/2 cup water
1/3 cup sugar
12 inches stick cinnamon, broken
1/2 teaspoon whole cloves
3 cups apple juice, chilled
1 can (12 ounces; 1 1/2 cups) apricot nectar, chilled
1/4 cup lemon juice

1. Combine water, sugar, cinnamon, and cloves in a saucepan. Bring to boiling. Reduce heat; simmer, covered, 10 minutes. Strain out spices; discard. Chill. Combine with apple juice, apricot nectar, and lemon juice. Makes 5 cups.

White Wine Punch: Prepare Party Punch Base. In a punch bowl, stir together the Party Punch Base and two 750-ml bottles of *chilled dry white wine*. Stir to mix. Makes 23 (4-ounce) servings.

Spiked Party Punch: Prepare Party Punch Base. In a punch bowl combine Party Punch Base with 2 cups *vodka*, *bourbon*, *brandy*, or *rum*. Stir to mix. Makes 14 (4-ounce) servings.

Individual Cocktails: Prepare Party Punch Base. For each cocktail, pour 1 jigger *vodka*, *bourbon*, *brandy*, or *rum* over ice in a cocktail glass. Add 1/2 cup Party Punch Base; stir. Makes 10 (4-ounce) servings.

Nonalcoholic Punch: Prepare Party Punch Base. Stir together the Base with two 28-ounce bottles (7 cups) of chilled *lemon-lime* or *grapefruit carbonated beverage*. Makes 22 (4-ounce) servings.

Quick Champagne Punch

See photo page 12.

1 can (6 ounces) frozen lemonade concentrate
1 bottle (750 milliliters; 3 cups) champagne, chilled
2 3/4 cups unsweetened pineapple juice, chilled
2 cups club soda, chilled
1 1/2 cups dry white wine, chilled
2 cups vanilla ice cream

1. Prepare lemonade in a large punch bowl according to package directions. Add champagne, pineapple juice, club soda, and wine. Top with scoops of vanilla ice cream. Stir gently before serving. Makes about 32 (4-ounce) servings.

Catawba Grape Punch

1 can (12 ounces) frozen lemonade concentrate, thawed
1 can (6 ounces) frozen apple juice concentrate, thawed
1 bottle (25.6 ounces) sparkling catawba grape juice, chilled
1 bottle (28 ounces) carbonated water, chilled

1. Combine concentrates in a 2-quart pitcher. Add grape juice and carbonated water, stirring gently to mix. Serve over ice. Makes 10 (6-ounce) servings.

*Daiquiri Punch makes
plenty for a party (double
the recipe for a crowd).
Omit the schnapps for a
nonalcoholic version.*

Daiquiri Punch

1 can (12 ounces) frozen orange juice concentrate, thawed
1 can (12 ounces) frozen pink lemonade concentrate, thawed
2 cans (6 ounces each) frozen strawberry daiquiri mix concentrate, thawed
2 cups peach or apricot nectar
1/3 cup peach schnapps
4 cans (12 ounces each) lemon-lime carbonated beverage, chilled
   Ice cubes *or* ice ring
   Strawberries (optional)

1. Combine concentrates and daiquiri mix in a punch bowl or large bowl. Stir in peach or apricot nectar, schnapps, and 2¼ cups *water*. Cover bowl; chill till serving time.
2. To serve, add carbonated beverage and ice cubes or ice ring. Float strawberries atop punch, if desired. Serve immediately. Makes about 15 cups or 20 (6-ounce) servings.

Bright Brunches

*R*ecognize the busy schedules everyone experiences
at holiday time. Greet your guests at a time of day that is
both accommodating and refreshing. It's a pleasure to host a brunch
with relaxed guests who linger over coffee. The menu choices
are endless; the occasions are memorable.

FRENCH ACCENT

*There's a New Orleans influence
in the menu (photo, left) which
includes Broiled Grapefruit,
Potato Omelet, Eggs Creole, Pain
Perdu, Bananas Foster, Ramos
Gin Fizz, Coffee, and Tea.*

Broiled Grapefruit

2   large grapefruit, halved
4   teaspoons honey
4   teaspoons margarine *or* butter
2   teaspoons sugar
    Dash ground cinnamon

1. Cut around sections of each grapefruit half. Spoon 1 teaspoon honey on each half. Top
each with 1 teaspoon of the margarine or butter. Sprinkle with sugar and cinnamon.
2. Broil 3 to 4 inches from heat about 2 minutes. Serve warm. Makes 4 servings.

Potato Omelet

¹/₂   cup chopped onion
¹/₄   cup cooking oil *or* shortening
  3   large potatoes, peeled and thinly sliced
  5   beaten eggs
      Dash salt
      Dash pepper

1. Cook chopped onion in hot cooking oil or shortening in a 10-inch skillet till tender
but not brown. Add sliced potatoes. Cover and cook about 18 minutes or till potatoes
are tender, stirring gently occasionally. Drain.
2. Add the beaten eggs to the skillet. Season with salt and pepper. Cook without
stirring till egg mixture begins to set on the bottom and around edges of the skillet.
Using a spatula, lift egg mixture so uncooked portion flows underneath. Cook about 3
minutes more or till eggs are cooked throughout but still glossy and moist.
3. Slide omelet onto a serving plate. Cut into wedges to serve. Makes 4 servings.

Eggs Creole

¹/₂ cup cooked and crumbled smoked sausage
¹/₄ cup shredded cheddar cheese
¹/₄ cup margarine *or* butter
¹/₂ teaspoon salt
2 cups cooked grits
1 green pepper, chopped
1 medium onion, chopped
2 stalks celery, chopped
2 cloves garlic, minced
1 bay leaf
2 tablespoons Worcestershire sauce
1 teaspoon paprika
1 teaspoon bottled hot pepper sauce
¹/₄ teaspoon dried thyme, crushed
1 can tomatoes (16 ounces), cut up
1 tablespoon cornstarch
¹/₄ cup cold water
1 beaten egg
¹/₄ cup milk
   All-purpose flour
   Soft bread crumbs
   Cooking oil
4 eggs

1. Stir sausage, cheese, 2 tablespoons margarine, and salt into hot cooked grits. Spoon into an 8x8x2-inch baking dish. Cover and chill till firm.
2. Melt remaining margarine in a large skillet. Add green pepper, onion, celery, and garlic. Cook and stir till nearly tender. Add bay leaf, Worcestershire sauce, paprika, hot pepper sauce, and thyme. Add *undrained* tomatoes. Simmer, covered, for 10 minutes.
3. Stir cornstarch into cold water; add to tomato mixture. Cook and stir till thickened and bubbly; cook and stir 2 minutes more. Discard bay leaf.
4. Cut chilled grits into four squares. In a shallow bowl stir together 1 egg and milk. Coat grit squares with flour, dip into egg mixture, and coat with bread crumbs. Fry in a small amount of hot oil till brown on both sides. Drain on paper towels; keep warm.
5. To poach eggs, grease a 2-quart saucepan. Add water to half-fill the saucepan. Bring water to boiling. Reduce heat to simmering. Break one egg into a shallow dish. Carefully slide egg into simmering water, holding the lip of the dish as close to the water as possible. Repeat with remaining eggs, allowing each egg an equal amount of space. Simmer, uncovered, for 3 to 5 minutes or till desired doneness. Remove eggs from water with a slotted spoon.
6. To serve, place grits on a platter; top with poached eggs and ladle sauce over the grits. Makes 4 servings.

2 tablespoons margarine *or* butter
¼ cup packed brown sugar
¼ teaspoon ground cinnamon
4 small bananas, sliced lengthwise
¼ cup light rum
1 tablespoon banana liqueur (optional)
French vanilla ice cream

1. Melt margarine or butter in a skillet or the blazer pan of a chafing dish over medium heat. Stir in brown sugar and cinnamon till dissolved. Add bananas; cook and stir for 3 to 4 minutes or till heated through.
2. Place rum and banana liqueur, if desired, in a small saucepan. Heat till almost simmering. (If desired, pour heated rum mixture into a large ladle.) Carefully ignite rum mixture with a long match. Pour over bananas and baste till flame burns out. Serve immediately over scoops of vanilla ice cream. Serves 4.

4 beaten eggs
2 cups milk
¼ cup sugar
¼ cup brandy
12 slices (1-inch thick) French bread
Cooking oil
Honey *or* maple syrup

1. Combine eggs, milk, sugar, and brandy in a shallow bowl; stir together well. Dip one slice of bread at a time into the egg mixture, soaking bread in mixture about 30 seconds on each side.
2. Cook bread slices in a large skillet or on a griddle in a small amount of hot oil for 2 to 3 minutes on each side or till brown. Pass honey or syrup. Serves 4.

1 cup crushed ice
½ cup milk, light cream, *or* half-and-half
3 ounces gin (6 tablespoons)
2 tablespoons Simple Syrup
4 teaspoons lemon juice
4 drops orange flower water
1 cup carbonated water, chilled

1. Combine ice, milk, gin, syrup, lemon juice, and flower water in a blender container. Cover and blend till frothy. Pour into four large glasses. Stir ¼ cup carbonated water into each glass. Serves 4.

Simple Syrup: Stir ½ cup boiling *water* into ½ cup *sugar* till sugar dissolves. Chill well. Store in the refrigerator.

A hearty brunch provides a jump start for a busy day. The menu includes Orange Muffins, Sausage and Apples, French Toast Strata, Cider Syrup, and Refrigerator Bran Muffins.

Orange Muffins

1 cup raisins *or* currants
1 cup sugar
1 cup margarine *or* butter, softened
2 tablespoons dairy sour cream
2 eggs
2 cups all-purpose flour
1/4 teaspoon salt
1 teaspoon baking soda
2/3 cup buttermilk
2 teaspoons finely shredded orange peel
1/3 cup sugar
1/4 cup orange juice

1. Grease eighteen 2$^{1}/_{2}$-inch muffin cups or line with paper bake cups. Set aside. If using raisins, place them in a food processor bowl. Cover and process raisins till finely chopped. (Or, use a knife to finely chop raisins.) Set aside.
2. Combine the 1 cup sugar, margarine, and sour cream in a medium bowl. Beat with an electric mixer on medium to high speed till fluffy. Beat in eggs.
3. Stir together flour and salt. Add flour mixture to margarine mixture, beating on low speed just till combined.
4. Stir baking soda into buttermilk. Stir buttermilk mixture into the batter just till combined. Fold in chopped raisins or currants and orange peel.
5. Spoon batter into the prepared muffin cups, filling each two-thirds full. Bake in a 400° oven for 14 to 15 minutes or till a toothpick inserted near each center comes out clean.
6. Meanwhile, in a small bowl stir together the 1/2 cup sugar and orange juice. Immediately brush the hot muffin tops with the orange juice mixture. Remove muffins from pans. Cool slightly on wire racks. Serve warm. Makes 18 muffins.

1 pound fresh pork sausage links
6 medium cooking apples (2 pounds total)
3 tablespoons brown sugar
1 tablespoon lemon juice
$^1/_4$ teaspoon salt
$^1/_8$ teaspoon pepper

1. Cook sausage in a 12-inch skillet over medium heat about 10 minutes or till no longer pink. Drain well and discard juices. Cut sausage links crosswise in half. Return sausage links to the skillet.
2. Core apples and cut each apple into eight wedges. Add apple wedges to sausage. Sprinkle with brown sugar, lemon juice, salt, and pepper.
3. Cover and cook over medium-low heat for 10 to 15 minutes or till apples are just tender, gently stirring once or twice. Makes 6 servings.

French
Toast Strata

1 loaf (1-pound) unsliced French bread
1 package (8 ounces) cream cheese, cubed
8 eggs
$2^1/_2$ cups milk, light cream, *or* half-and-half
6 tablespoons margarine *or* butter, melted
$^1/_4$ cup maple syrup *or* maple-flavor syrup
Cider Syrup

1. Cut French bread into cubes. (You should have about 12 cups bread cubes.)
2. Grease a 3-quart rectangular baking dish. Place *half* of the bread cubes in the dish. Top with cream cheese cubes and remaining bread cubes.
3. Combine eggs, milk, melted margarine or butter, and maple syrup in a blender container or a mixing bowl. Process or beat with a rotary beater till well combined. Pour egg mixture evenly over bread and cheese cubes. Using a spatula, slightly press layers down to moisten. Cover with plastic wrap and refrigerate for 2 to 24 hours.
4. Remove plastic wrap from baking dish. Bake, uncovered, in a 325° oven for 35 to 40 minutes or till the center appears set and the edges are lightly golden. Let stand about 10 minutes before serving. Serve with Cider Syrup. Makes 6 to 8 servings.

Cider
Syrup

$^1/_2$ cup sugar
4 teaspoons cornstarch
$^1/_2$ teaspoon ground cinnamon
1 cup apple cider *or* apple juice
1 tablespoon lemon juice
2 tablespoons margarine *or* butter

1. Combine sugar, cornstarch, and cinnamon in a small saucepan. Stir in apple cider or apple juice and lemon juice.
2. Cook and stir the mixture over medium heat till thickened and bubbly. Cook and stir for 2 minutes more.
3. Remove saucepan from heat and stir in margarine or butter till melted. Makes about $1^1/_3$ cups.

Refrigerator Bran Muffins

1¹/4 cups all-purpose flour
1¹/4 teaspoons baking soda
 ¹/4 teaspoon salt
1¹/2 cups whole bran cereal
 ¹/2 cup boiling water
   1 beaten egg
   1 cup buttermilk
 ³/4 cup sugar
 ¹/4 cup cooking oil
 ¹/2 cup raisins

1. In a medium mixing bowl stir together flour, baking soda, and salt. Set mixture aside.
2. Place *¹/2 cup* of the bran cereal in a small mixing bowl. Pour the boiling water over the cereal and set aside.
3. Combine egg, buttermilk, sugar, cooking oil, and the remaining bran cereal in a large mixing bowl. Add flour mixture to egg mixture. Stir just till moistened. Add the soaked bran and stir just till well combined. Fold in raisins.
4. Transfer batter to a covered container. Refrigerate overnight or up to 3 days.
5. To bake, grease twelve 2¹/2-inch muffin cups or line muffin cups with paper bake cups. Spoon batter into the prepared cups, filling each two-thirds full. Bake in a 400° oven for 15 to 20 minutes or till tops spring back when lightly touched. Remove from pans; cool slightly on wire racks. Serve warm. Makes 12.

Caramel-Apple Pandowdy

   5 medium McIntosh, Rome Beauty, *or* Granny Smith apples, peeled, cored, and thinly sliced (5 cups)
 ³/4 cup packed brown sugar
 ¹/2 cup margarine *or* butter
   1 cup all-purpose flour
1¹/2 teaspoons baking powder
 ¹/8 teaspoon salt
 ¹/8 teaspoon ground cinnamon
 ¹/8 teaspoon ground nutmeg
 ¹/8 teaspoon ground allspice
 ¹/2 cup sugar
   1 egg
 ¹/2 cup applesauce
 ¹/4 cup raisins
 ¹/4 cup chopped pecans
      Light cream (optional)

1. Arrange apple slices evenly in a 2-quart square baking dish. Top with brown sugar. Dot with *¹/4 cup* of the margarine.
2. In a mixing bowl stir together flour, baking powder, salt, cinnamon, nutmeg, and allspice. Set aside.
3. Place remaining margarine in another mixing bowl. Beat with an electric mixer for 30 seconds. Beat in sugar. Beat in egg. Add flour mixture and applesauce alternately to the beaten mixture, beating well. Stir in raisins and pecans. Spoon batter evenly over the apples.
4. Bake in a 350° oven for 35 to 40 minutes or till a toothpick inserted into the cake topping comes out clean. Serve warm. Pass light cream, if desired. Makes 8 servings.

1/2 pound sliced bacon
1/2 cup packed brown sugar
  1 teaspoon ground cinnamon

1. Cut bacon slices in half crosswise. Let bacon come to room temperature.
2. Combine sugar and cinnamon. Coat each bacon slice with sugar mixture. Twist bacon slices and place in a shallow baking pan. Bake in a 350° oven for 15 to 20 minutes or till crisp and sugar is bubbly. (Watch closely; sugar burns easily.) Drain well.
3. Place cooked bacon on foil to cool. Serve at room temperature. Serves 8.

Sugar-Crust Bacon

TRADITIONS

Serve a legendary brunch with a menu which includes Caramel-Apple Pandowdy, Sugar-Crust Bacon, Orange Marmalade Muffins, Potato Patties, Easy Eggs Benedict, Citrus Mimosa and Coffee with Liqueurs.

  2 cups all-purpose flour
  1 cup sugar
3/4 teaspoon baking powder
  2 beaten eggs
  1 cup dairy sour cream
1/4 cup orange marmalade
  1 tablespoon margarine *or* butter, melted
11/2 teaspoons vanilla

1. Grease twelve 21/2-inch muffin cups or line with paper bake cups.
2. Stir together flour, sugar, and baking powder in a medium mixing bowl. Make a well in the center.
3. Combine eggs, sour cream, marmalade, melted margarine or butter, and vanilla in another bowl. Add sour-cream mixture all at once to the flour mixture. Stir just till moistened.
4. Fill the muffin cups two-thirds full. Bake in a 400° oven for 20 to 25 minutes or till tops are golden. Remove muffins from pan and cool slightly on wire rack. Serve warm. Makes 12 muffins.

Orange-Marmalade Muffins

Potato Patties

4   cups cold mashed potatoes
1/2 cup light cream *or* milk
12   soda crackers, crushed (about 1/2 cup crumbs)
1   small onion, finely chopped
1   slightly beaten egg
1/4 teaspoon celery salt
1/4 teaspoon pepper
1/8 teaspoon garlic salt
     Tomato wedges and parsley (optional)

1. Combine potatoes, cream or milk, cracker crumbs, onion, egg, celery salt, pepper, and garlic salt in a mixing bowl. Stir together well.
2. Shape potato mixture into twelve 1/2-inch-thick patties. Cook on a greased,* preheated griddle over medium heat or in an electric skillet at 350° for 3 to 4 minutes or till brown on the underside and warm on top. Turn and cook 3 to 4 minutes more or till brown. Keep warm in a 300° oven while cooking remaining potato patties.
3. Serve the warm potato patties garnished with tomato wedges and parsley, if desired. Makes 12 patties.
* **Note:** For crispier potato patties, fry in more cooking oil or shortening.

Easy Eggs Benedict

3/4 cup margarine *or* butter
3/4 cup all-purpose flour
6   cups milk
1   pound fully cooked ham, cut into cubes
1   cup shredded cheddar cheese
8   hard-cooked eggs, quartered
1   pound fresh *or* frozen asparagus spears, cut into 1-inch pieces and cooked
1   tablespoon sherry (optional)
8   squares (3 inches) corn bread

1. For sauce, melt margarine in a large saucepan. Stir in flour. Add milk all at once. Cook and stir till thickened and bubbly. Cook and stir 1 minute more.
2. Add ham and cheese to sauce. Cook and stir on low till blended. Add eggs, asparagus, and sherry, if desired. Stir gently. Season with salt and pepper.
3. To serve, ladle sauce over warm corn-bread squares. Makes 8 servings.

Hot Cider Sauce

3/4 cup apple cider *or* apple juice
1/2 cup packed brown sugar
1/2 cup light corn syrup
2   tablespoons margarine *or* butter
1/2 teaspoon lemon juice
1/8 teaspoon ground cinnamon
1/8 teaspoon ground nutmeg

1. Combine apple cider or apple juice, brown sugar, corn syrup, margarine, lemon juice, cinnamon, and nutmeg in a medium saucepan. Cook and stir over medium heat till sugar dissolves and mixture is bubbly.
2. Simmer mixture about 20 minutes more or till reduced to 1 cup, stirring occasionally. Let stand 30 minutes before serving to thicken slightly. Makes 1 cup.

2 tablespoons Irish cream liqueur
1 1/2 tablespoons amaretto
1 1/2 tablespoons Frangelico liqueur
   Hot coffee
   Whipped cream
   Maraschino cherry with stem

1. Place liqueurs in a coffee cup or tall glass coffee mug. Pour in hot coffee. Top with whipped cream and a cherry. Makes 1 serving.

1 cup prepared strawberry daiquiri mix
1 can frozen orange juice concentrate (6 ounces), thawed
3/4 cup water
1/3 cup fresh grapefruit juice
1/2 of a 6-ounce can (1/3 cup) frozen lemonade concentrate, thawed
3 tablespoons frozen limeade concentrate, thawed
   Chilled champagne
   Thin orange slices, halved

1. Combine prepared daiquiri mix, orange juice concentrate, water, grapefruit juice, lemonade concentrate, and limeade concentrate in a pitcher or bowl. Stir till well combined. Cover and chill.
2. To serve, pour the chilled juice mixture into eight ice-filled glasses, filling each glass half full. Pour an equal amount of the chilled champagne into each glass. Garnish with orange slice halves. Makes 8 (6-ounce) servings.

1 cup all-purpose flour
1 tablespoon sugar
2 teaspoons baking powder
1/2 teaspoon salt
1/2 teaspoon ground cinnamon
1 cup milk
1/2 cup canned pumpkin
2 slightly beaten egg yolks
2 tablespoons cooking oil
2 egg whites

1. Combine flour, sugar, baking powder, salt, and cinnamon in a large mixing bowl. In another mixing bowl combine milk, pumpkin, egg yolks, and cooking oil. Add pumpkin mixture to flour mixture all at once. Stir just till blended.
2. Beat egg whites till stiff peaks form (tips stand straight). Gently fold beaten egg whites into pumpkin mixture.
3. Pour about 1/4 cup batter onto a hot, lightly greased griddle or heavy skillet for each pancake. Cook till pancakes are golden brown, turning to cook second sides when pancakes have bubbly surfaces and slightly dry edges.
4. Serve with Hot Cider Sauce (recipe, left). Makes fourteen 4-inch pancakes.

Beautiful Buffets

*For relaxed hosting and comfortable guests,
nothing outshines the buffet. Platters of tempting foods
call people to serve themselves. The plates don't need to match—
mixed dinnerware adds to the festivities. From gourmet delicacies to
simple, hearty soups, the buffet is a great way to serve
a lunch, supper, or dinner party.*

---

2   packages (9 ounces each) frozen artichoke hearts *or* 2 pounds fresh
        baby artichokes
2   tablespoons olive oil *or* cooking oil
2   teaspoons instant chicken bouillon granules
$1/2$ teaspoon dried tarragon, crushed
$1/4$ teaspoon garlic powder
$1/8$ teaspoon black pepper
$1/4$ cup chopped sweet red pepper
1   tablespoon lemon juice

1. Thaw frozen artichokes (wash fresh artichokes, cut off stems and $1/2$ inch of tops, and pull off coarse outer leaves).
2. Cook artichokes in hot oil in a large skillet about 5 minutes for thawed artichokes (10 minutes for fresh artichokes) or till tender, carefully turning occasionally. Remove skillet from the heat.
3. Add bouillon granules, tarragon, garlic powder, black pepper, and 1 cup *water*. Bring to boiling; reduce heat. Simmer, covered, about 5 minutes for thawed artichokes (12 to 15 minutes for fresh artichokes) or till tender. Stir in chopped red pepper and lemon juice. Cool. Transfer to a bowl; cover and chill overnight.
4. To serve, bring artichoke mixture to room temperature. Drain and transfer to a serving bowl. Makes 8 servings.

Marinated Artichokes

TEXTURE

A variety of shapes and textures increases the appeal of your buffet dishes. The photo, left, includes Marinated Artichokes, Calcutta Meatballs, and Tomato-Cheese Crostini.

Calcutta Meatballs

1/2 cup light raisins
1/2 cup pine nuts, lightly toasted
1/4 cup thinly sliced green onions
1 teaspoon ground cinnamon
1/2 teaspoon ground allspice
2 cloves garlic, minced
1 pound ground lamb *or* ground beef
Fresh marjoram (optional)
Plain yogurt

1. Combine raisins and pine nuts in a food processor bowl or blender container. Process till just finely chopped.
2. Stir together raisin mixture, onions, cinnamon, allspice, garlic, and 1/2 teaspoon *salt* in a bowl. Add lamb or beef. Mix well. Shape into 1-inch balls. Arrange meatballs in a shallow baking pan. Bake in a 350° oven 12 to 15 minutes or till no pink remains, turning once.
3. Drain on paper towels. Garnish with sprigs of fresh marjoram, if desired. Serve hot with yogurt. Makes about 36.

Country Pork Platter

2 slices thick-cut bacon, cut into 1-inch pieces
1 large onion, chopped (1 cup)
2 medium carrots, sliced (1 cup)
2 cloves garlic, minced
1/2 cup dry white wine
2 tablespoons packed brown sugar
1 tablespoon vinegar
1/2 teaspoon salt
1/4 teaspoon pepper
6 cups shredded cabbage
2 red *and/or* green apples, cored and cubed
10 juniper berries (optional)
3/4 pound fully cooked smoked bratwurst, knockwurst, frankfurters, *and/or* smoked sausage links, cut in half
6 fully cooked smoked boneless pork chops, cut 1/2 inch thick (about 2 pounds)
6 small potatoes, boiled

1. In a 4-square Dutch oven cook bacon till crisp. Remove bacon with a slotted spoon. Add onion, carrots, and garlic to Dutch oven. Cook and stir 5 minutes. Stir in wine, brown sugar, vinegar, salt, and pepper. Stir in cabbage, apples, bacon pieces, and juniper berries, if desired. Bring mixture to boiling. Cover. Reduce heat and simmer 25 to 30 minutes. Transfer the mixture to large bowl; cover and chill up to 2 days.
2. Return cabbage mixture to Dutch oven. Nestle sausage pieces and pork chops into mixture. Heat to boiling; reduce heat and simmer, covered, about 30 minutes or till chops are heated through. Transfer to a large platter. Serve with hot boiled potatoes. Makes 6 servings.

1 unsliced French bread baguette, frozen
3 tablespoons olive oil
8 ounces goat cheese with herbs, shredded
2 cups shredded mozzarella cheese (8 ounces)
3/4 cup ricotta cheese (8 ounces)
1 clove garlic, minced
  Dash white pepper
6 sun-dried tomato halves (oil pack), cut into thin strips

1. Slice bread into 1/4-inch-thick slices. Place bread on baking sheets; brush tops with oil. Bake in 300° oven about 12 minutes or till golden brown. Remove from the oven. Increase oven temperature to 350°.
2. Meanwhile, in large bowl combine goat cheese, mozzarella, ricotta cheese, garlic, and white pepper. Blend well.
3. Spread each bread slice with some of the cheese mixture. Top with tomato strips and return to oven. Bake about 3 minutes or till cheese begins to melt. Serve warm. Makes about 40.

Tomato-Cheese Crostini

1 medium onion, chopped (1/2 cup)
2 cloves garlic, minced
2 tablespoons olive or cooking oil
1/4 cup all-purpose flour
1/2 teaspoon dried basil or oregano, crushed
1/4 teaspoon salt
2 cups milk
1/4 cup grated Parmesan or Romano cheese
1 can (14 ounces) artichoke hearts, drained and cut up
2 tablespoons snipped parsley
2 to 4 tablespoons milk (optional)
8 ounces fettuccine, cooked and drained
  Snipped parsley
  Coarsely ground pepper

1. For sauce, in a saucepan cook onion and garlic in oil till tender. Stir in flour, basil or oregano, and salt. Add 2 cups milk all at once. Cook; stir till thickened and bubbly. Cook; stir 1 minute more. Stir in cheese; transfer to a container. Cover; refrigerate for up to 24 hours.
2. To serve, transfer sauce to a medium saucepan. Stir in the artichoke hearts and 2 tablespoons parsley; heat through. If sauce is too thick, stir in enough additional milk to make of desired consistency. Spoon sauce over hot fettuccine. Sprinkle with additional fresh parsley and pepper. Makes 8 side-dish servings.

Fettuccine with Artichoke Sauce

*A circle of red pepper pieces
decorates this easy-to-make
Bacon and Onion Tart.*

Bacon and Onion Tart

¹/₂ of a 15-ounce package folded refrigerated unbaked pie crusts (1 crust)
  6 slices bacon, diced
  3 medium onions, thinly sliced and separated into rings
  3 slightly beaten eggs
  1 cup light cream *or* half-and-half
¹/₂ teaspoon dry mustard
¹/₈ teaspoon pepper
   Roasted red sweet peppers, cut into bite-size pieces*
   Snipped parsley

1. Let pie crust stand at room temperature according to package directions.
2. Roll piecrust, if necessary, into a 12-inch circle on a lightly floured surface. Ease the pastry into an ungreased 10-inch tart pan. Press pastry into fluted sides of tart pan and trim edges.
3. Line the pastry shell with a double thickness of foil. Bake in a 450° oven for 5 minutes. Remove foil. Bake for 5 to 7 minutes more or till pastry is nearly done; set aside. Reduce oven temperature to 325°.
4. Meanwhile, for filling, in a large skillet cook the bacon till crisp. Remove bacon, reserving 2 tablespoons drippings in skillet. Drain bacon on a paper towel. Cook onion, covered, in the reserved drippings over medium heat about 5 minutes or till onion is tender but not brown, stirring occasionally.
5. Combine the eggs, light cream or half-and-half, dry mustard, and pepper in a medium mixing bowl. Arrange the onion in an even layer in the prebaked pastry shell. Sprinkle with the bacon. Pour the egg mixture over the onion and bacon in the pastry shell.
6. Bake in the 325° oven about 25 minutes or till a knife inserted near the center comes out clean. Let stand for 15 minutes before serving. Garnish with roasted pepper and snipped parsley. Cut into 16 wedges. Makes 16 servings.

  * Roasted Peppers: You may purchase roasted red sweet peppers in a jar at your supermarket, or you can roast your own. To roast, halve peppers and remove seeds and membranes. Place the peppers, cut side down, on a foil-lined baking sheet. Bake in a 425° oven about 20 minutes or till skins are browned and bubbly. Then place the peppers in a new brown paper bag; seal and let stand about 20 minutes or till cool enough to handle. Peel skin from peppers.

   5 cups torn leaf lettuce, romaine, Bibb *or* Boston lettuce, *and/or* spinach
   1 cup shredded carrot
   1 cup broccoli *or* cauliflower flowerets
   1 medium cucumber, peeled, halved lengthwise, and thinly sliced
 1/2 cup reduced-calorie mayonnaise *or* salad dressing
 1/3 cup plain low-fat yogurt
   1 teaspoon Dijon-style mustard
 1/4 teaspoon dried dillweed *or* basil, crushed
 1/8 teaspoon cracked black pepper
   2 to 3 tablespoons milk
 1/2 of a small red onion, thinly sliced and separated into rings

1. Place torn lettuce and/or spinach in the bottom of a deep glass bowl. Then layer carrot, broccoli or cauliflower, and cucumber on top.
2. For dressing, stir together mayonnaise, yogurt, mustard, dillweed or basil, and pepper in a bowl. Add enough milk to make of desired consistency. Spread dressing over top of salad. Cover and refrigerate for up to 24 hours.
3. To serve, garnish with onion rings and fresh dill, if desired. Serves 8.

   1 pound bulk Italian sausage
   1 package (10 ounces) frozen chopped spinach, thawed and well drained
   1 can (8 ounces) tomato sauce
   1 can (4 ounces) sliced mushrooms, drained
 1/3 cup fine dry seasoned bread crumbs
   1 jar (2 ounces) sliced pimiento, drained
   1 loaf (16 ounces) frozen whole wheat *or* rye bread dough, thawed
   1 tablespoon margarine *or* butter, melted

1. For filling, in a large skillet cook sausage till brown; drain well. Add spinach, tomato sauce, mushrooms, bread crumbs, and sliced pimiento. Mix thoroughly. Set aside.
2. For crust, on a lightly floured surface roll *two-thirds* of the bread dough into an 11-inch circle. Carefully place circle in a greased 9-inch springform pan, patting dough 1 inch up the sides. Add filling.
3. On the lightly floured surface, roll the remaining dough into a 10-inch circle. Cut circle into 10 to 12 wedges. Arrange wedges atop sausage filling, slightly overlapping edges and sealing ends to bottom crust along edge of the pan. Brush top with melted margarine or butter.
4. Bake in a 375° oven for 30 to 35 minutes or till crust is golden brown. If necessary, cover top with foil the last 10 minutes to prevent overbrowning. Cool on a wire rack for 10 minutes. Remove sides of the pan. Cut into wedges to serve. Serve warm. Makes 10 to 12 appetizer servings.

Wild-Rice Braid

1 cup water
¹/3 cup wild rice
3³/4 to 4¹/4 cups all-purpose flour
2 packages active dry yeast
³/4 cup milk
¹/4 cup margarine *or* butter
¹/4 cup honey
1 teaspoon salt
1 beaten egg
2 small tart apples, peeled and finely chopped (1 cup)
1 beaten egg yolk
1 tablespoon water

1. Bring water to boiling in a small saucepan. Add rice. Return to boiling; reduce heat. Cover and simmer 40 to 50 minutes or till rice is done. Let cool.
2. Stir together *1¹/2 cups* of the flour and yeast in a large mixer bowl. In a saucepan heat milk, margarine or butter, honey, and salt till warm (120° to 130°) and margarine almost melts, stirring constantly. Add to flour mixture; add egg. Beat with an electric mixer on low speed for 30 seconds, scraping sides of the bowl. Beat on high speed for 3 minutes. Stir in rice and apples. Using a wooden spoon, stir in as much of the remaining flour as you can.
3. Turn dough out onto lightly floured surface. Knead in enough of the remaining flour to make a moderately stiff dough that is smooth and elastic (about 6 to 8 minutes total). Shape dough into a ball. Place in a greased bowl, turning once. Cover and let rise in a warm place till double (about 1 hour).
4. Punch dough down; turn out onto a long counter that is lightly floured. Divide dough in half. Divide each half into three portions. Cover dough; let rest for 10 minutes.
5. Roll each portion of dough into a 26-inch rope. Lightly grease two baking sheets. Place three ropes, side by side, on a baking sheet (ropes will extend beyond edges of baking sheets). Braid ropes loosely, starting at the center and working toward ends. Avoid stretching dough. Shape braid into a figure eight around balls of foil; tuck ends of braid under in the center. Repeat with remaining ropes of dough. Cover and let rise till nearly double (about 40 minutes).
6. Combine egg yolk and 1 tablespoon water. Brush on braids. Bake in a 375° oven for 25 to 30 minutes or till done, covering with foil after 15 to 20 minutes to prevent overbrowning. Cool on wire rack. Makes 2 loaves, 24 servings.

Black-Bean Salad

2 cans (15 ounces each) black beans
1 can (16 ounces) whole kernel corn, drained
1 large green pepper, cut into thin strips 1 inch long (1 cup)
2 medium tomatoes, seeded and cut into ¹/2-inch pieces
1 cup sliced celery
¹/2 cup sliced green onion
¹/2 cup Italian salad dressing
¹/2 cup hot picante salsa
Romaine (optional)
¹/2 of a small onion, sliced and separated into rings

1. Drain black beans; rinse and drain. In a large bowl combine beans, corn, pepper, tomatoes, celery, green onion, salad dressing, and picante salsa. Cover and chill 4 to 48 hours. Stir once or twice. If desired, serve in a romaine-lined salad bowl. Top with onion slices. Makes 16 servings.

Homemade soup and bread create a relaxing and delicious buffet supper. Vegetable Oyster Stew and Wild-Rice Braid make it luxurious as well.

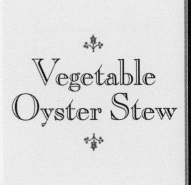

Vegetable Oyster Stew

- 2 medium potatoes, peeled and cubed
- 1 large onion, chopped
- 3/4 cup water
- 1 teaspoon instant chicken bouillon granules
- 1/2 teaspoon salt
- 1/4 teaspoon pepper
- 2 medium carrots, thinly sliced (1 cup)
- 1 cup broccoli flowerets
- 1 pint shucked oysters
- 2 cups milk
- 1 cup light cream
  Margarine *or* butter (optional)

1. Combine potatoes, onion, water, bouillon granules, salt, and pepper in a 3-quart saucepan. Bring to boiling. Reduce heat; simmer, covered, for 12 minutes. Add carrots and broccoli; simmer, covered, 10 minutes more.

2. Add *undrained* oysters; cook, uncovered, over medium heat about 5 minutes or till edges of oysters curl, stirring frequently. Add milk and cream; heat through but do not boil. If desired, place a small pat of margarine or butter atop each serving. Makes 6 servings.

Chicken Caviar Crepes

32 Mini Savory Crepes
1 package (9 ounces) frozen diced cooked chicken, thawed
1/2 cup honey-Dijon ranch salad dressing
1/4 cup snipped parsley
   Leaf lettuce (optional)
1 jar (2 ounces) red *or* gold caviar

1. Thaw Mini Savory Crepes, if frozen. Finely chop the chicken. In a medium bowl combine the chicken, salad dressing, and parsley. Place a scant tablespoon of the chicken mixture in the center of *unbrowned* side of crepe. Fold in two sides on a slight diagonal to each other to form a cornucopia shape.
2. Line a serving platter with lettuce, if desired. Arrange filled crepes over lettuce. Spoon a small amount of caviar on top of each crepe. Makes 32 servings.

Mini Savory Crepes

1. In a bowl combine 1 1/2 cups *milk*; 1 cup *all-purpose flour*; 2 *eggs*; 1 tablespoon *cooking oil*; 1/2 teaspoon *fine herbes* or *dried oregano*, crushed; and 1/4 teaspoon *salt*. Beat with a rotary beater until well mixed.
2. Heat a lightly greased 6-inch skillet. Remove from heat. Spoon *1 tablespoon* of the batter into center of skillet. Allow batter to spread to a 4-inch circle. Return skillet to heat. Brown the crepe on one side only, about 45 seconds or till the batter is set.
3. Run a spatula around edge of crepe to loosen. Invert skillet and remove crepe. Repeat with remaining batter, lightly greasing skillet as necessary.
4. Use crepes immediately or store in a covered container with 4-inch square of waxed paper between crepes. Store in refrigerator 2 days or in the freezer up to 1 month. Makes 32.

IMPRESSIVE

Herbed crepes are rolled cornucopia-style around chicken filling and decorated with caviar for these Chicken Caviar Crepes.

1¹/4 cups orange juice
1 package (3 ounces) raspberry- *or* strawberry-flavor gelatin
1 cup cranberry-orange, cranberry-raspberry, *or* cranberry-strawberry sauce
1 cup whipping cream
1 cup chopped pear *or* apple (1 medium)
Lettuce leaves
Orange slices (optional)

1. Bring orange juice to boiling in a medium saucepan; remove from heat. Add gelatin, stirring till dissolved. Stir in cranberry-orange, cranberry-raspberry, or cranberry-strawberry sauce. Chill till partially set (the consistency of unbeaten egg whites).
2. Beat whipping cream in a chilled small mixing bowl till soft peaks form. Fold whipped cream and pear into partially set gelatin. Chill till mixture mounds when dropped from a spoon.
3. Spoon gelatin mixture into a lightly oiled 4-cup ring mold. Chill for at least 6 hours or till firm.
4. To serve, dip mold into warm water for a few seconds to loosen edges. Center a lettuce-lined plate upside down over the mold. Hold the mold and plate together and invert them. Shake the mold gently till salad loosens; carefully lift off mold. Garnish with orange slices, if desired. Makes 6 servings.

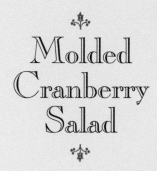

Molded Cranberry Salad

4 slices bacon
¹/2 cup chopped onion
1 can (10³/4 ounces) cream of potato soup
¹/2 cup milk
¹/8 teaspoon pepper
2 cups thinly sliced peeled potatoes
2 cups thinly sliced peeled sweet potatoes

1. Cook bacon till crisp; drain, reserving *1 tablespoon* bacon drippings. Crumble bacon and set aside. Cook onion in reserved drippings till tender. Stir in soup, milk, and pepper.
2. Set aside several slices of potato. In a greased 1¹/2-quart casserole arrange *one-third* of the remaining potatoes, *one-third* of the sweet potatoes, and *one-third* of the bacon. Pour about *one-third* of the soup mixture over potatoes. Repeat twice, arranging reserved potato slices in center of final sweet potato layer, and ending with the last of the soup mixture.
3. Bake covered, in 350° oven for 60 minutes or in 325° oven for 1 hour 10 minutes. Uncover; bake 10 to 15 minutes more or till done. Makes 8 servings.

Two-Potato Scallop

Gala Holiday Dinners

❦

*H*onor great traditions and launch new ones when you serve glorious holiday meals. While everything is better when wrapped with the Christmas spirit, these recipes provide ways to embellish your menu and make the occasion even more memorable. Beautiful birds, dressed, sauced, and roasted till golden, as well as glazed ham or tender beef will announce your festive holiday celebration.

❦

2 Cornish game hens (1 to 1¹/2 pounds each)
   Wild Rice Stuffing
   Melted margarine *or* butter

1. Halve the Cornish hens lengthwise. Rinse hen halves. Twist wing tips under backs. Cover and chill.
2. To bake, spoon Wild-Rice Stuffing into 4 mounds on bottom of a 13x9x2-inch baking dish. Place Cornish hens, cut side down, over rice mounds in pan. Brush with melted margarine.
3. Bake, covered, in a 375° oven for 45 minutes. Uncover. Brush hens with melted margarine or butter. Bake, uncovered 30 to 45 minutes more or till tender. Arrange hens atop rice stuffing on four plates. Makes 4 servings.
   Wild-Rice Stuffing: In a medium saucepan cook ¹/2 cup *chopped onion* in 1 tablespoon *margarine* or *butter* till tender. Stir in 1³/4 cups *chicken broth*; ¹/2 cup *wild rice*; ¹/4 cup regular *brown rice*; ¹/4 teaspoon *ground sage*, ¹/4 teaspoon *dried oregano*, crushed; and ¹/8 teaspoon *pepper*. Bring to boiling; reduce heat. Simmer, covered, for 40 to 50 minutes or till liquid is absorbed. Stir in 1 cup shredded *carrot*. Cool; cover and chill up to 24 hours.

❦

Game Hens with Wild-Rice Dressing

❦

SMALLER PARTIES

Enjoy big impact for your small dinner when you serve Game Hens with Wild Rice Dressing or Roast Duck with Kumquat Sauce (both shown in photo, left).

Roast Duck with Kumquat Sauce

1 domestic duckling (4 to 5 pounds)
Kumquat Sauce

1. Rinse duck and pat dry. Tuck drumsticks under the band of skin across the tail. Skewer neck skin to back. Twist wing tips under back. Prick skin well all over. Place bird, breast side up, on a rack in a shallow roasting pan. Insert a meat thermometer into thigh meat. Roast, uncovered in a 375° oven for 1³/4 to 2¹/4 hours or till meat thermometer registers 180° to 185°. Remove fat during roasting. Cover; let stand 15 minutes. If desired, garnish duck with lemon leaves and additional kumquats. Pass Kumquat Sauce. Makes 6 servings.

Kumquat Sauce: Thinly slice 3 *preserved kumquats*, removing seeds. In a small saucepan combine ¹/2 cup *water*, ¹/3 cup *orange juice*, 1 tablespoon *cornstarch*, and 1 teaspoon instant *chicken bouillon granules*. Cook and stir till bubbly; cook and stir 2 minutes more. Add kumquats, 2 tablespoons toasted chopped *pecans*, and 1 tablespoon *orange liqueur*; heat through.

Bourbon-Sauced Pheasant

1 cup snipped mixed dried fruit
1 can (5¹/2 ounces) apricot nectar
¹/3 cup bourbon
3¹/2 cups bread cubes (about 5 slices)
¹/2 cup chopped pecans
¹/2 teaspoon ground cinnamon
3 tablespoons margarine *or* butter, melted
2 domestic pheasants (2 pounds each)
2 slices bacon, halved crosswise
¹/4 cup plum jelly

1. In a small saucepan mix dried fruit, nectar, and bourbon. Bring to boiling. Reduce heat; cover and simmer 5 minutes. Remove from heat. Let stand 15 minutes. Drain; reserve liquid.
2. Meanwhile, place bread cubes in large shallow baking pan. Toast in a 375° oven 10 to 15 minutes or till dried. In a large mixing bowl combine bread, nuts, and cinnamon. Drizzle with margarine and *¹/4 cup* reserved liquid. Toss lightly till well mixed. Stir in fruit.
3. Rinse birds; pat dry. Season cavities with *salt*. Skewer neck skin to backs. Spoon stuffing into body cavities. Tie legs to tails. Twist wing tips under.
4. Place birds, breast side up, on rack in shallow roasting pan. Lay bacon over breasts. Roast in a 350° oven 1¹/4 to 1¹/2 hours or till done. Measure remaining stuffing. For each cup, stir in 1 tablespoon *water*. Place in casserole; cover and chill. Add covered casserole to oven the last 30 minutes of roasting.
5. In a small saucepan heat and stir jelly with remaining reserved liquid till jelly melts. Discard bacon; baste pheasant frequently with plum sauce the last 15 minutes. Cover birds; let stand 15 minutes before carving. Makes 8 servings.

1 domestic goose (8 to 10 pounds)
2 tablespoons lemon juice
3/4 cup apple-cherry juice
1/3 cup sugar
9 inches stick cinnamon
6 whole cloves
1 tablespoon cornstarch
1 package (16 ounces) frozen unsweetened pitted tart red cherries, thawed and
      drained, *or* one 16-ounce can pitted tart red cherries (water pack), drained
2 tablespoons brandy *or* Kirsch

1. Rinse goose; pat dry. Season cavity with *salt*. Tuck drumsticks under the band of skin across the tail. Skewer neck skin to back. Twist wing tips under back. Prick skin well.
2. Place bird, breast side up, on a rack in a roasting pan. Brush with lemon juice. Insert a meat thermometer into the thigh meat. Roast, uncovered, in a 350° oven 2³/4 to 3¹/4 hours or till meat thermometer registers 180° to 185°. Remove fat during roasting. Cover; let stand for 15 minutes before carving.
3. Meanwhile, mix juice, sugar, cinnamon, and cloves. Bring to boiling. Reduce heat; cover and simmer for 15 minutes. Remove the spices. Combine cornstarch and 1 tablespoon *cold water*; add to juice mixture. Cook and stir till bubbly; cook and stir 2 minutes more. Add cherries and brandy; heat through. Pass sauce. Serves 10.

Cherry
Roasted
Goose

   Lime Poppy Seed Dressing
   Leaf lettuce *or* spinach
3 pears, sliced into thin wedges
1 tablespoon lemon juice
2 cups seedless green and/or red grapes, halved
1/2 cup broken walnuts

1. Prepare Lime Poppy Seed Dressing (recipe follows).
2. Line 8 salad plates with leaf lettuce or spinach. In a medium bowl toss pear wedges with lemon juice.
3. Arrange pear wedges, grapes, and walnuts atop leaf lettuce on each salad plate. Cover and chill till serving time, up to 1 hour. Drizzle with Lime Poppy Seed Dressing. Makes 8 servings.

Lime
Poppy Seed
Fruit Salad

1/3 cup honey
1/4 teaspoon finely shredded lime peel
3 tablespoons lime juice
1¹/2 teaspoons poppy seed
1/8 teaspoon ground mace
1/4 cup salad oil
2 tablespoons walnut oil *or* salad oil

1. In a small mixer bowl stir together honey, lime peel, lime juice, poppy seed, mace and 1/4 teaspoon *salt*. Beat with electric mixer on medium-high speed while gradually adding oils. Continue beating till mixture thickens.
2. Cover and chill. Stir before serving. After chilling, if mixture is too thick to drizzle, let stand at room temperature for 30 minutes. Makes 3/4 cup.

Lime
Poppy Seed
Dressing

Traditional with all the trimmings, this dinner includes Roast Turkey and Chestnut Stuffing, Cherry-Thyme Sauce, Winter Fruits with Balsamic Vinaigrette, and Colonial Green Beans.

Winter Fruits with Balsamic Vinaigrette

1/4 cup salad oil
1/4 cup orange juice
3 tablespoons balsamic vinegar
1 tablespoon honey
1/8 teaspoon cracked pepper
2 medium pink grapefruit
1 medium orange
2 medium pears, cored and cut into wedges
2 teaspoons lemon juice
1 head red *and/or* green leaf lettuce
1 cup red *and/or* green seedless grapes

1. For dressing, in a blender container or food processor bowl combine salad oil, orange juice, vinegar, honey, and pepper. Cover and blend or process till combined. Cover and chill till serving time.
2. Use a small, sharp knife to peel grapefruit and orange, removing as much of the white membranes as possible. Section grapefruit and cut orange crosswise into 8 slices. Brush pear wedges with lemon juice.
3. Cover a large platter with lettuce leaves. Arrange grapefruit sections, orange slices, pear wedges, and grapes atop lettuce. Cover the platter with plastic wrap and chill for up to 4 hours. Before serving, drizzle with dressing. Makes 8 side-dish servings.

8 ounces fresh chestnuts *or* one 4-ounce package dried chestnuts
   1 cup thinly sliced celery
   1 large onion, chopped
 $^{1}/_{2}$ cup margarine *or* butter
   1 teaspoon dried thyme, crushed
 $^{1}/_{4}$ teaspoon pepper
   1 loaf (16 ounces) French *or* Italian bread, cut into $^{1}/_{2}$-inch cubes and toasted*
 $1^{1}/_{2}$ cups chicken broth
 $^{1}/_{4}$ cup water
 $^{1}/_{4}$ cup dry vermouth, sherry, *or* chicken broth
   1 turkey (14 to 16 pounds)
     Cooking oil *or* melted butter
     Red apple wedges (optional)
     Fresh sage *and/or* thyme sprigs (optional)
     Cherry-Thyme Sauce (recipe, page 84)

Roast Turkey and Chestnut Stuffing

1. For stuffing, if using fresh chestnuts, cut an X in the flat side of *each* chestnut, using a small, sharp knife. Place the chestnuts in a large saucepan and cover with cold water. Bring to boiling and reduce heat. Cover and simmer for 10 to 15 minutes. Drain. When chestnuts are cool enough to handle, peel and chop. If using dried chestnuts, cook according to package directions and chop.

2. Meanwhile, in a small saucepan cook celery and onion in hot margarine or butter till tender but not brown. Stir in thyme and pepper. In a large bowl combine chestnuts and bread cubes; stir in celery mixture. Drizzle with broth, water, and vermouth or sherry; toss gently to coat.

3. Rinse turkey, then pat dry. Season body cavity with *salt*. Spoon some of the stuffing loosely into neck cavity. Skewer neck skin to back. Spoon more stuffing loosely into body cavity (do not pack stuffing too tight or it will not get hot enough by the time the turkey is cooked). Tuck drumsticks under tail skin or tie to tail. Twist wing tips under the back. Transfer any remaining stuffing to a casserole; cover and chill.

4. Place turkey, breast side up, on a rack in a shallow roasting pan. Brush with oil or butter. Insert a meat thermometer into the center of one of the inside thigh muscles. The bulb should not touch the bone. Cover turkey loosely with foil. Roast turkey in a 325° oven for $4^{1}/_{2}$ to $5^{1}/_{2}$ hours or till thermometer registers 180° to 185°. Cut band of skin between legs after $3^{1}/_{2}$ hours. Bake casserole of stuffing alongside turkey for the last 40 to 45 minutes of cooking time. Uncover the bird the last 30 minutes of roasting. When done, remove turkey from oven and cover. Let stand 20 minutes before carving.

5. To serve, use a spoon to remove stuffing from turkey. Place stuffing in a serving bowl. If carving the whole turkey at the table, transfer to a serving platter. If desired, garnish with apple wedges and sage and/or thyme sprigs. Serve Cherry-Thyme Sauce with turkey and stuffing. Makes 12 to 14 servings.

*Note: To toast bread cubes, spread cubes in a single layer in a $15^{1}/_{2}$x$10^{1}/_{2}$x2-inch baking pan. Bake in a 300° oven for 10 to 15 minutes or till dry, stirring twice.

Cherry-Thyme Sauce

1 cup unsweetened cherry juice
3/4 cup chicken broth
1/2 cup dried cherries, snipped
1/4 cup finely chopped onion
1 teaspoon dried thyme, crushed
1 teaspoon white wine Worcestershire sauce
1/2 to 1 teaspoon sugar
1/8 teaspoon pepper
1/4 cup unsweetened cherry juice
4 teaspoons cornstarch

1. In a small saucepan stir together the 1 cup cherry juice, chicken broth, dried cherries, onion, thyme, white wine Worcestershire sauce, sugar, and pepper. Bring to boiling over medium-high heat; reduce heat. Cover and simmer for 15 minutes. Stir together the 1/4 cup cherry juice and cornstarch. Stir into cherry mixture. Cook and stir till thickened and bubbly. Cook and stir 2 minutes more. Serve warm with turkey. Makes 2 cups.

Colonial Green Beans and Bacon

7 slices bacon
2 packages (9 ounces each) frozen Italian-style green beans, thawed
6 medium carrots, thinly sliced
2 tablespoons margarine *or* butter
2 cloves garlic, minced
1/2 teaspoon pepper

1. In a large skillet cook the bacon, uncovered, over medium heat for 8 to 10 minutes or till just crisp, turning occasionally. Remove bacon, reserving drippings; drain on paper towels.
2. Drain all but *2 tablespoons* of the bacon drippings from the skillet. Add green beans, carrots, margarine or butter, and garlic. Stir-fry over medium-high heat about 5 minutes or till vegetables are crisp-tender. Crumble bacon, leaving 1 strip whole for a garnish, if desired. Stir crumbled bacon and pepper into vegetable mixture. Remove from heat. Transfer to a serving bowl. If desired, top with the reserved bacon slice. Makes 8 servings.

Hot Curried Fruit

1 can (16-ounce) *each* peach slices *and* pear slices, drained
1 can (15 1/2 ounces) pineapple chunks, drained
1 can (8 3/4 ounces) unpeeled apricot halves, drained
2 tablespoons margarine *or* butter, melted
1/3 cup packed brown sugar
1/2 teaspoon curry powder
1/4 cup walnuts

1. Arrange drained fruit in a 1 1/2-quart casserole. Combine butter, brown sugar, and curry powder. Spoon over fruit. Bake in a 325° oven for 40 to 45 minutes or till bubbly around the edges. Sprinkle with walnuts. Makes 8 servings.

You'll be a star when you serve Orange-Honey Glazed Ham served with Hot Curried Fruit.

  1 lower-sodium fully cooked boneless ham (2 to 2$^1/_2$ pounds)
$^1/_4$ cup orange juice
  2 tablespoons honey
  1 tablespoon mustard
$^1/_4$ cup chicken broth
  2 teaspoons cornstarch
$^1/_3$ cup orange marmalade

1. Make diagonal cuts about $^1/_4$ inch deep and 1 inch apart on the top of ham. Place ham on rack in shallow baking pan. Insert a meat thermometer in the center of the thickest portion of meat. Bake, uncovered, in a 325° oven 1$^1/_2$ to 2 hours or till thermometer registers 140°.

2. Meanwhile, combine *2 tablespoons* of the orange juice, the honey, and mustard. Bring to boiling; remove from heat. After ham has baked about 1$^1/_4$ hours, brush with *half* the glaze.

3. Mix remaining orange juice, chicken broth, and cornstarch. Stir into remaining glaze. Cook and stir till thickened and bubbly. Cook and stir 2 minutes more. Stir in marmalade; heat through. Pass with sliced ham. Serves 8 to 10.

Orange-
Honey
Glazed
Ham

Filet of Beef

1 beef tenderloin roast (3 pounds)
1/4 cup country-style Dijon mustard
1 tablespoon coarsely ground black pepper
Mustard Sauce Dijon (recipe follows)
Fresh herbs (optional)

1. Spread beef tenderloin with mustard and sprinkle with pepper. Fold the thin end of tenderloin under to make of uniform thickness. Place beef on a rack in a shallow roasting pan. Bake in a 425° oven for 50 to 60 minutes or till a meat thermometer registers 140° (for rare). Remove roast from oven.
2. If serving warm, tent with foil and let it stand 10 minutes before slicing. Or, cover and chill up to 48 hours and serve cold. Garnish with fresh herbs, if desired. Serve with Mustard Sauce Dijon. Makes 8 servings.

OPTIONS
────────

For a sit-down dinner or a buffet; served hot or cold, Filet of Beef with Mustard Sauce Dijon, Salade Niçoise and Lemon Champagne Sorbet make an elegant menu.

Mustard Sauce Dijon

1/4 cup finely chopped shallots *or* onion
1 tablespoon margarine *or* butter
1 tablespoon all-purpose flour
1 cup beef broth
1/3 cup country-style Dijon mustard
2 tablespoons brandy
1 tablespoon chili sauce

1. In a medium saucepan cook shallots or onion in margarine or butter till tender. Stir in flour. Cook and stir till flour just begins to brown. Carefully add beef broth. Cook and stir till thickened and bubbly. Cook and stir 1 minute more. Add mustard, brandy, and chili sauce; stir till well mixed. Cover and chill.
2. Serve cold with cold roast beef or warm with hot roast beef. To reheat, cook over medium heat, stirring frequently, for 2 to 3 minutes or till hot. Makes about 1¹/₂ cups.

3 tablespoons white wine vinegar
2 tablespoons snipped parsley
1 teaspoon fresh tarragon *or* oregano, snipped
1/2 teaspoon garlic salt
1/2 teaspoon dry mustard
1/2 cup olive oil
1 package (16 ounces) frozen whole green beans
2 packages (9 ounces each) frozen artichoke hearts
1 pound small red potatoes
1 head Boston *or* bibb lettuce
4 small tomatoes
24 pitted ripe olives
1/2 cup crumbled blue cheese
2 tablespoons chopped red onion

1. In a jar with a tight lid combine vinegar, parsley, tarragon or oregano, garlic salt, and mustard. Close and shake till salt is dissolved. Add oil, close, and shake till blended. Set aside.

2. Cook beans and artichoke hearts according to package directions. Drain; place in covered container and chill. Cook potatoes in lightly salted boiling *water* 20 minutes or till tender. Drain. Cool 15 minutes. Peel and slice 1/4 inch thick. Place potatoes in a shallow bowl or casserole. Shake dressing and pour about *1/4 cup* over potatoes. Cover. Pour remaining dressing over beans and artichokes. Cover. Chill vegetables 4 to 24 hours, stirring occasionally.

3. About 2 hours before dinner, line 8 individual salad plates or a large platter with lettuce. Cut tomatoes into 8 wedges each. Arrange tomatoes, potatoes, green beans, artichokes, and olives on plates or platter. Sprinkle with cheese and chopped onion. Cover and chill till serving time. Serves 8.

1/2 cup sugar
1 envelope unflavored gelatin
1 cup water
2/3 cup light corn syrup
1 teaspoon finely shredded lemon peel
2 cups champagne *or* white wine
1 cup light cream
1/4 cup lemon juice
Few drops yellow food coloring

1. In a medium saucepan combine sugar and unflavored gelatin. Add water and corn syrup. Cook and stir over medium heat till sugar and gelatin dissolve. Remove from heat.

2. Add the lemon peel, champagne or wine, light cream, lemon juice, and yellow food coloring. (Mixture will look curdled.)

3. Freeze in a 4- to 5-quart ice cream freezer according to manufacturer's directions. Or place mixture in a 9x9x2-inch baking pan. Cover and freeze for 2 to 3 hours or till almost firm. Transfer mixture to a chilled bowl. Beat with an electric mixer till smooth but not melted. Return to baking pan. Cover and freeze till firm. Makes about 1 1/2 quarts (12 servings).

Delightful Desserts

✤

*E*nd on a sweet note when you present the finale

to a holiday evening. Or, skip the dinner invitation and entertain

guests who "come for dessert." The urge to splurge is satisfied

in style when you share these sweet specialties.

✤

Almond Biscotti Bites

✤

1/3 cup margarine *or* butter
2/3 cup sugar
2 teaspoons baking powder
2 eggs
2 teaspoons finely shredded orange *or* lemon peel
1 teaspoon vanilla
2 cups all-purpose flour
1 1/2 cups slivered almonds *or* hazelnuts (filberts), very finely chopped
1 beaten egg yolk
1 tablespoon milk
6 ounces semisweet chocolate, chopped
1 tablespoon shortening
Ground almonds *or* hazelnuts (filberts)

1. Beat margarine or butter in a mixing bowl with an electric mixer on medium to high speed for 30 seconds. Add sugar and baking powder and beat till combined. Beat in eggs, orange or lemon peel, and vanilla till combined. Beat in as much of the flour as you can with the mixer. Stir in any remaining flour and chopped nuts.
2. Shape dough into three 14-inch rolls. Place rolls about 3 inches apart on a lightly greased cookie sheet. Slightly flatten to 3/4-inch thickness. Combine egg yolk and milk; brush egg-yolk mixture on rolls. Bake in a 375° oven for 15 to 20 minutes or till lightly browned. Cool on cookie sheet for about 1 hour.
3. Cut each cookie roll into 1/4-inch-thick slices. Lay slices, cut sides down, on an ungreased cookie sheet. Bake in 325° oven 5 minutes. Turn slices over; bake 5 to 10 minutes more or till dry and crisp. Remove cookies; cool on rack.
4. Melt chocolate and shortening in a small saucepan over low heat, stirring often to avoid scorching. Dip half of each cookie into the chocolate. Allow excess chocolate to drip off; roll cookie in ground nuts. Place cookies on waxed paper; let stand till chocolate is firm. Makes about 120.

JUST A BITE

Gold candy cups and a gold doily glamorize your presentation of these little sweets (photo, left). Shown are Almond Biscotti Bites, Strawberries with Crème Fraîche, Double-Dipped Fruits, and Glazed Nuts.

Double-Dipped Fruits

2 to 3 cups medium strawberries, maraschino cherries with stems, dried apricots, *or* candied pineapple wedges
4 ounces white baking bar, chopped
1 tablespoon shortening
4 ounces semisweet chocolate, chopped
1 tablespoon shortening

1. Gently wash strawberries, if using, leaving stems and hulls attached. Pat completely dry with paper towels. If using maraschino cherries, drain and pat completely dry with paper towels. Set the fruit aside.
2. Melt the white baking bar and 1 tablespoon shortening in a small heavy saucepan over low heat, stirring often to avoid scorching.
3. To dip, place one piece of fruit on the end of a wooden skewer, if necessary, or grasp fruit by stem. Dip *half* of each piece of fruit diagonally into the melted white baking bar. Allow excess to drip off; place fruit on waxed paper. Let stand till firm.
4. Melt the semisweet chocolate with 1 tablespoon shortening in a small heavy saucepan over low heat, stirring often to avoid scorching. Dip *half* of each piece of fruit diagonally into the melted chocolate, leaving about half of the white dipping exposed. Allow the excess chocolate to drip off; place the fruit on waxed paper. Let stand till chocolate is firm.
5. Serve the fruit the same day it is dipped. Makes about 1$^{1}/_{2}$ pounds.

Strawberries with Crème Fraîche

18 large or 24 medium strawberries *or* 24 large Medjool dates
1 package (8 ounces) cream cheese, softened
$^{1}/_{4}$ cup sifted powdered sugar
Crème Fraîche
1 tablespoon finely crushed Glazed Nuts (recipe, page 91) or finely chopped toasted almonds

1. Gently wash and hull strawberries. Pat completely dry with paper towels. Place strawberries, stem ends down, on a cutting board. Cut each from the top to, but not through, the stem end. Repeat to cut each strawberry into four wedges. Slightly spread wedges apart. Set strawberries aside. If using dates, cut a lengthwise slit in each date. Remove pits. Slightly spread each date apart. Set aside.
2. For filling, beat cream cheese and powdered sugar in a small mixing bowl with an electric mixer on medium to high speed till combined. Fold in $^{1}/_{4}$ *cup* Crème Fraîche. (Store remaining Crème Fraîche, covered, in the refrigerator for up to 1 week; serve over fresh fruit.)
3. Spoon filling into a decorating bag fitted with a medium star or round tip (about $^{1}/_{4}$-inch opening). Pipe filling into each strawberry or date. Sprinkle tops with crushed Glazed Nuts or finely chopped almonds. Chill in the refrigerator till serving time or for up to 2 hours. Makes 18 or 24.

   Crème Fraîche: Stir together $^{1}/_{4}$ cup *whipping cream* (not ultrapasteurized) and $^{1}/_{4}$ cup *dairy sour cream* in a mixing bowl. Cover with plastic wrap. Let stand at room temperature for 2 to 5 hours or till mixture thickens. When thickened, cover and chill in the refrigerator till serving time or for up to 1 week. Stir before serving. Makes $^{1}/_{2}$ cup.

   Note: Crème Fraîche recipe may be doubled or quadrupled.

Margarine *or* butter
1¹/₂ cups blanched whole almonds, hazelnuts (filberts), macadamia nuts, walnut
         halves, *or* pecan halves
  ¹/₂ cup sugar
  2 tablespoons margarine *or* butter
  ¹/₂ teaspoon vanilla

1. Line a baking sheet with foil. Grease foil with margarine; set aside. In a heavy
10-inch skillet combine nuts, sugar, the 2 tablespoons margarine or butter, and vanilla.
2. Cook over medium-high heat, shaking skillet occasionally, till sugar begins to melt.
(Do not stir.) Reduce heat to low; cook till sugar is melted and golden brown, stirring
frequently. Remove from heat. Pour onto the prepared baking sheet. Cool completely.
3. Break nuts into clusters. Cover tightly; store in a cool, dry place for up to 1 month.
Makes about 2 cups.
   Individual Glazed Nuts: Prepare Glazed Nuts as above except, after removing the
skillet from the heat, use a well-buttered spoon to remove a few nuts at a time.
Working quickly, separate the nuts on the foil. Cool and store as directed above.

  2 teaspoons margarine *or* butter
  ¹/₄ cup ground almonds
  16 ounces white baking bar with cocoa butter, chopped
  4 packages (8 ounces each) cream cheese, softened
  ¹/₂ cup margarine *or* butter, softened
  3 tablespoons milk
  1 tablespoon vanilla
      Dash salt
  4 eggs
  1 egg yolk
  4 bars (1¹/₂ ounces each) milk chocolate with almonds, chopped
      Chocolate curls (optional)

1. Grease bottom and sides of a 10-inch springform pan with the 2 teaspoons margarine
or butter. Press ground almonds onto the bottom of the pan. Set pan aside.
2. Heat and stir the white baking bar in a heavy medium saucepan over low heat *just
till melted*. In a large mixing bowl beat melted baking bar, cream cheese, the ¹/₂ cup
margarine or butter, milk, vanilla, and salt with an electric mixer on medium to high
speed till combined. Add whole eggs and egg yolk all at once. Beat on low speed *just till
combined*. Stir in chopped milk chocolate.
3. Pour filling into the prepared springform pan. Bake cheesecake on a shallow baking
pan in a 375° oven for 45 to 50 minutes or till the cheesecake appears *nearly* set in the
center when the pan is gently shaken.
4. Cool cheesecake in the springform pan on a wire rack for 10 minutes. Using a small
metal spatula, loose cheesecake from sides of the pan. Cool for 30 minutes more.
Remove side of springform pan. Cool completely; chill at least 4 hours. If desired,
garnish with chocolate curls. Makes 16 servings.

Lady Baltimore Cake or Cranberry-Raisin Pie could become a traditional dessert — once served, always remembered.

Lady Baltimore Cake

2¹/₂ cups all-purpose flour
2 cups sugar
1 teaspoon baking powder
1 teaspoon finely shredded orange peel
¹/₂ teaspoon baking soda
¹/₈ teaspoon salt
1¹/₃ cups buttermilk *or* sour milk
¹/₂ cup shortening, margarine, *or* butter, softened
1 teaspoon vanilla
4 egg whites
1 cup raisins
8 dried figs, snipped (¹/₂ cup)
¹/₄ cup brandy
1 cup toasted chopped pecans
¹/₃ cup finely chopped candied red *or* green cherries
¹/₃ cup finely chopped candied pineapple *or* mixed candied fruits and peels
Seven-Minute Frosting (recipe, page 93)

1. In a bowl stir together flour, sugar, baking powder, orange peel, baking soda, and salt. Add buttermilk, shortening, and vanilla. Beat for 30 seconds, scraping sides of bowl. Beat for 2 minutes, scraping bowl often. Add egg whites; beat for 2 minutes more, scraping bowl.
2. Pour batter into 3 greased and floured 8x1¹/₂-inch round baking pans; spread evenly. Bake in a 350° oven about 30 minutes or till a toothpick inserted near center comes out clean. Cool for 10 minutes. Loosen from sides; remove from pans. Cool on wire racks. (At this point, you may cover and freeze the cake for up to 6 months.)
3. For filling, in a medium bowl combine raisins, figs, and brandy; let stand at room temperature about 2 hours or till brandy is absorbed, stirring occasionally. Stir in pecans, fruits, and about *one-third (1¹/₃ cups)* of the Seven-Minute Frosting.
4. To assemble, place one cake layer on a platter; spread *half* of the filling on top. Add another cake layer and the remaining filling. Top with the remaining cake layer. Frost with the remaining frosting. Serve within 2 hours. Makes 12 servings.

1¹/2 cups sugar
¹/3 cup cold water
2 egg whites
¹/4 teaspoon cream of tartar *or* 2 teaspoons light corn syrup
1 teaspoon vanilla

1. In the top of a double boiler combine sugar, cold water, egg whites, and cream of tartar or corn syrup. Beat for 30 seconds or till mixed.
2. Place over boiling water (upper pan should not touch water). Cook, beating constantly with the electric mixer on high speed, about 7 minutes or till frosting forms stiff peaks. Remove from heat; add vanilla. Beat for 2 to 3 minutes more or till frosting is of spreading consistency.

¹/4 cup margarine *or* butter
1 cup chopped cranberries
1 cup chopped raisins
1 cup sugar
3 tablespoons all-purpose flour
1 teaspoon vanilla
Pastry for Lattice-Top Pie
Coarse sugar

1. For filling, combine ¹/2 cup *boiling water* and margarine; stir till melted. Stir in cranberries, raisins, sugar, flour, and vanilla. Set aside.
2. On a floured surface, flatten *one ball* of pastry dough. Roll from center to edges, forming a 12-inch circle. Transfer to a 9-inch pie plate. Ease into plate, without stretching. Trim to ¹/2 inch beyond edge. Roll remaining dough into a 10-inch circle. Cut into ¹/2-inch-wide strips.
3. Spread filling in pastry. Weave strips atop to make a lattice top. Press ends of strips into rim of crust. Fold bottom pastry over strips; seal and flute edge. Sprinkle with coarse sugar. Cover edge with foil. Bake in 375° oven for 25 minutes. Remove foil; bake for 20 to 25 minutes more or till crust is golden. Cool on a wire rack. Makes 8 servings.
   Pastry for Lattice-Top Pie: In a bowl stir together 2 cups *all-purpose flour* and ¹/2 teaspoon *salt*. Cut in ²/3 cup *shortening* or *lard* till pieces are size of small peas. Sprinkle 1 tablespoon of *cold water* over part of mixture; gently toss with a fork. Push to side of bowl. Repeat with 5 to 6 more tablespoons *cold water* till all is moistened. Divide dough in half. Form each half into a ball.

Buttermilk Chocolate Cake

(See cover photo.)

2 cups all-purpose flour
1³/4 cups sugar
1 teaspoon baking powder
1 teaspoon baking soda
¹/4 teaspoon salt
1¹/3 cups buttermilk *or* sour milk
¹/2 cup shortening
1 teaspoon vanilla
2 eggs
3 squares (3 ounces) unsweetened chocolate, melted and cooled
Butter Frosting (recipe follows)
Chocolate Curls
Fresh raspberries *or* frozen unsweetened raspberries, thawed and drained

1. Grease and lightly flour two 9x1¹/2-inch round baking pans; set aside. In a large bowl, stir together flour, sugar, baking powder, baking soda, and salt. Add buttermilk, shortening, and vanilla.
2. Beat with an electric mixer on low speed 30 seconds or till combined. Beat on medium to high speed 2 minutes; scrape bowl occasionally. Add eggs and melted chocolate; beat 2 minutes.
3. Pour batter into pans. Bake in a 350° oven 30 to 35 minutes or till cakes test done. Cool in pans 10 minutes. Remove cakes from pans; cool completely.
4. Frost with Butter Frosting. Decorate with Chocolate Curls and raspberries.

   Chocolate Curls: Make curls with *milk chocolate bars* or *white baking bars with cocoa butter* (white chocolate). With chocolate bar at room temperature, carefully draw a vegetable peeler at an angle across the bar. For small curls, use the narrow side of the bar; for large curls, use the wide side.

Butter Frosting

¹/3 cup butter *or* margarine
4¹/2 cups sifted powdered sugar
¹/4 cup milk
1¹/2 teaspoons vanilla
Milk (optional)

1. Beat butter or margarine in a large mixing bowl with an electric mixer on medium to high speed till light and fluffy. Gradually add *2 cups* of the powdered sugar, beating well on low to medium speed. Slowly beat in the ¹/4 cup milk and vanilla.
2. Gradually beat in the remaining powdered sugar. If necessary, beat in additional milk to make a frosting of spreading consistency. Makes enough for sides and tops of two 8- or 9-inch cake layers or the top of one 13x9-inch cake.

Make Holiday Ice-Cream Bombe up to a month ahead. If you don't have a mold, use a large freezerproof bowl lined with plastic wrap.

Holiday Ice-Cream Bombe

 3 cups pistachio ice cream *or* mint chocolate-chip ice cream
 3 cups vanilla ice cream
 1/2 cup diced mixed candied fruits and peels
 1 quart chocolate *or* chocolate-fudge ice cream
   Pistachio nuts (optional)
   Chocolate Leaves (optional)
   Chocolate Sauce

1. In a chilled mixing bowl stir pistachio ice cream just to soften. Spread evenly in the bottom of a 2-quart mold. Freeze for 30 minutes.
2. Meanwhile, in a chilled mixing bowl stir vanilla ice cream just to soften. Stir in candied fruits and peels. Spread evenly over pistachio ice-cream layer. Freeze for 30 minutes.
3. In a chilled mixing bowl stir chocolate ice cream just to soften. Spread evenly over vanilla ice-cream layer. Cover and freeze for at least several hours or up to 1 month.
4. To serve, wrap a hot damp towel around mold for several seconds. Center an upside-down serving platter over the mold. Holding tightly, invert the plate and mold. Lift off the mold. Garnish with pistachio nuts and Chocolate Leaves, if desired. Serve at once with Chocolate Sauce. Serves 10.

Chocolate Leaves: In a heavy saucepan cook 2 squares (2 ounces) *semisweet chocolate* over low heat till the chocolate begins to melt, stirring constantly. Immediately remove the chocolate from the heat and stir till smooth. With a small paintbrush, brush melted chocolate on the underside of nontoxic fresh leaves (such as lemon, mint, or ivy), building up layers of chocolate so garnish will be sturdy. Wipe off chocolate that may have run onto the front of the leaves. Place on a baking sheet lined with waxed paper; chill or freeze till hardened. Just before using, carefully peel the fresh leaves away from the chocolate leaves.

Chocolate Sauce: In a small saucepan combine 8 squares (8 ounces) *semisweet chocolate*, cut up, and 2/3 cup *light cream*. Cook over medium-low heat till slightly thickened and bubbly. Remove from heat. Stir in 1 teaspoon *vanilla*. Serve warm. Makes 1 cup.

1¹/₂ cups all-purpose flour
3 tablespoons granulated sugar
3 tablespoons finely chopped almonds
¹/₂ teaspoon salt
¹/₃ cup cooking oil
3 tablespoons milk
1 can (16 ounces) whole cranberry sauce
1 tablespoon cornstarch
1 tablespoon cranberry liqueur *or* raspberry liqueur
1¹/₂ cups white baking pieces
1 egg
2 tablespoons water
¹/₄ teaspoon almond extract
2 cups whipping cream
2 tablespoons powdered sugar
1 teaspoon vanilla
Toasted slivered almonds (optional)

1. Combine flour, *1 tablespoon* of the granulated sugar, the chopped almonds, and the salt in a bowl. Combine oil and milk; stir into flour mixture. Press onto bottom and sides of a 9-inch pie plate. Prick crust with a fork. Bake in a 400° oven 12 to 14 minutes. Cool.

2. Combine cranberry sauce, cornstarch, and remaining granulated sugar in a saucepan. Cook and stir till bubbly; cook 1 minute more. Stir in liqueur. Cool.

3. For candy filling, in a small saucepan melt white baking pieces over low heat; remove from heat. Slightly beat egg and water. Gradually stir *half* of the melted pieces into the egg. Add egg mixture to saucepan; cook and stir over medium heat 7 minutes or till thickened. Remove from heat. Stir in almond extract; cool.

4. Beat whipping cream, powdered sugar, and vanilla with electric mixer till soft peaks form; reserve *half*. Fold remainder into candy mixture. Spoon *half* of the candy filling into pie shell. Reserve *¹/4 cup* cranberry mixture; spread remaining mixture over candy filling. Top with remaining candy filling. Decorate with reserved whipped cream and cranberry mixture. If desired, sprinkle with almonds. Chill for up to 8 hours. Makes 8 servings.

STRIPED CANDY

Cranberry Ribbon Pie is a Christmas surprise package — a candy layer with pretty red decorations.

3 slices white bread
1 beaten egg
3/4 cup dairy eggnog
3/4 cup all-purpose flour
3/4 teaspoon baking soda
1/2 teaspoon ground nutmeg
2/3 cup packed brown sugar
1/2 cup margarine *or* butter, cut up
2 tablespoons rum *or* brandy
2 cups raisins
1/2 cup chopped walnuts
  Sugared Orange-Peel Curls (optional)
3 tablespoons rum *or* brandy (optional)
  Rum Hard Sauce (optional)

1. Tear bread into pieces. Combine egg, bread, and eggnog; let stand 3 minutes or till softened. In another bowl combine flour, baking soda, and nutmeg. Lightly grease a 6-cup mold or heatproof mixing bowl; set aside.
2. Stir bread mixture to break up pieces. Stir in brown sugar, margarine, and the 2 tablespoons rum. Stir in raisins and nuts. Add flour mixture; stir till combined. Pour bread mixture into prepared mold or bowl. Cover with foil, pressing tightly against rim. Place on a rack in a deep kettle. Pour *boiling water* into the kettle around the mold till water covers 1 inch of the mold. Cover the kettle. Bring water to a gentle boil.
3. Steam, adding more boiling water as necessary, about 2 1/2 hours or till a wooden skewer inserted near the center of the pudding comes out clean.
4. Carefully remove mold or bowl from kettle. Cool on a rack for 10 minutes. Invert pudding onto a serving platter; remove the mold or bowl. If desired, garnish with orange-peel curls. If desired, in a saucepan heat the 3 tablespoons rum or brandy till hot. Ignite with a long match and pour over pudding. Serve after flame goes out. If desired, serve with Rum Hard Sauce. Serves 8 to 10.

  To make ahead: Prepare and steam pudding as directed above. Unmold, cool on a rack, and wrap tightly in foil. Store in the refrigerator for up to 1 week. To reheat, place the foil-wrapped pudding on a baking sheet. Heat in a 350° oven for about 40 minutes or till heated through. Serve as directed above.

  Sugar Orange-Peel Curls: Cut long strips of orange peel. Twist into curls; coat well with sugar. Let stand on waxed paper to dry. Store in a cool, dry place for up to 1 week.

  Rum Hard Sauce: In a bowl combine 1 cup sifted *powdered sugar* and 1/4 cup *margarine* or *butter,* softened. Beat with an electric mixer on medium speed for 3 to 5 minutes or till combined. Beat in 1 tablespoon *rum* or *brandy.* Cover and chill about 3 hours or till firm.

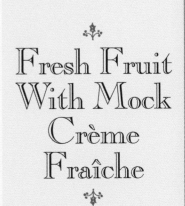

1 carton (8 ounces) vanilla yogurt
1 container (8 ounces) fruit-flavor, soft-style cream cheese
1 cup carambola slices (also called star fruit)
5 cups cut-up fresh fruit, such as seedless red or green grapes, kiwi fruit, strawberries, pears, bananas, *and/or* oranges

1. Combine yogurt and cream cheese in a small mixing bowl. Beat with an electric mixer on low speed till combined. Arrange carambola and an assortment of the fresh fruit on 8 dessert plates. Spoon a dollop of the yogurt mixture on each dessert plate; sprinkle with *cinnamon.* Makes 8 servings.

Among My Favorite Things

*Traditional treats make memories.
Cookies, candies, and breads are as much a part of
Christmas as lights on the tree and stockings
hung at the fireplace.
Cookie buildings and cookie creatures are included
here, as are special recipes that make great gifts.
Making the recipes in this chapter can become a
family tradition, as enjoyable as the finished
products. The cookie baking and decorating and
the all-important tasting duties become family
activities. Shared activity in the kitchen,
beating the candy, savoring the accompanying
aromas, and sampling the products is an ideal
recipe for good memories.
Wrap up a gift from your kitchen. You'll find gift-
giving specialties in the chapter Giftbasket Foods.
Other chapters in this section also offer ideas for
cookies and candies and breads to share.
These special edible treats are fun to prepare
and wonderful to give.*

Cookies For Santa

❖

Christmas without cookies is like a puppy without a wagging tail. Happiness seems to drift through the house when a sheet of cookies comes out of the oven. The activity of making and sharing cookies may be every bit as wonderful as eating these traditional treats.

❖

1/2 cup margarine *or* butter
1/2 cup shortening
1 1/2 cups all-purpose flour
1 cup sugar
1 cup packed brown sugar
2 eggs
1 1/2 teaspoons ground cinnamon
1 teaspoon baking soda
1 teaspoon vanilla
1/2 teaspoon salt
3 cups quick-cooking rolled oats
1/2 cup finely chopped black walnuts *or* walnuts

1. Beat margarine or butter and shortening in a bowl with an electric mixer on medium to high speed for 30 seconds or till softened. Add about *half* of the flour, the sugar, brown sugar, eggs, cinnamon, baking soda, vanilla, and salt. Beat till thoroughly combined, scraping sides of bowl occasionally. Then beat or stir in remaining flour. Stir in oats and nuts.
2. Shape dough into two 10-inch rolls; wrap each in waxed paper or clear plastic wrap. Chill for 4 to 24 hours.
3. Cut dough into 1/4-inch slices. Place 1 inch apart on an ungreased cookie sheet.
4. Bake in a 375° oven for 7 to 9 minutes or till edges are lightly browned. Cool on the cookie sheet for 1 minute. Remove cookies and cool on a wire rack. Makes about 70.

Oatmeal-Nut Crisps

❖

FLAVORS

Spices, fruits, and nuts flavor the temptations shown (left) on the plate: Sand Tarts, Oatmeal-Nut Crisps, and Spicy Holiday Fruit Bars; on the silver server: Hermits and Gramma Carey's Tea Tarts.

Spicy Holiday Fruit Bars

2 cups all-purpose flour
1 teaspoon ground cinnamon
1/2 teaspoon ground ginger
1/2 teaspoon baking soda
1/2 teaspoon ground nutmeg
1/4 teaspoon ground cloves
1/4 teaspoon ground allspice
1/2 cup shortening
1/2 cup packed brown sugar
3/4 cup buttermilk
1/3 cup molasses
1 egg
1/2 cup chopped nuts
1/3 cup raisins, chopped dates, dried cherries, *or* dried cranberries
1/3 cup chopped mixed candied fruit and peels
Orange Icing
Additional mixed candied fruit and peels (optional)

1. Stir together the flour, cinnamon, ginger, baking soda, nutmeg, cloves, and allspice in a bowl; set aside.
2. Beat shortening in a large mixing bowl with an electric mixer on medium to high speed for 30 seconds. Add brown sugar; beat till fluffy. Add buttermilk, molasses, and egg. Gradually add flour mixture, beating till combined. Stir in nuts, raisins, and 1/3 cup candied fruit.
3. Spread in a greased 15x10x1-inch baking pan. Bake in a 350° oven for 15 to 20 minutes or till lightly browned. Cool thoroughly in pan on wire rack. Frost with Orange Icing. Decorate with additional candied fruit and peels, if desired. Cut into bars. Makes 48.

Orange Icing: Stir together 2 cups sifted *powdered sugar*, 1 teaspoon finely shredded *orange peel*, 1/2 teaspoon *vanilla*, and enough *orange juice* (about 2 tablespoons) to make icing of spreading consistency.

Gramma Carey's Tea Tarts

1/3 cup margarine *or* butter
1 package (3 ounces) cream cheese, softened
1 cup all-purpose flour
2 tablespoons sugar
1/4 cup fruit preserves
Chocolate Glaze (optional)

1. Beat margarine or butter and cream cheese in a mixing bowl with an electric mixer on medium to high speed about 30 seconds or till softened. Add flour and sugar. Beat till well mixed. Form dough into a ball.
2. Roll dough, half at a time, into a 10x7 1/2-inch rectangle on a lightly floured surface. Cut into 2 1/2-inch squares. Spoon about *1/2 teaspoon* preserves onto center of each. Moisten edges of each pastry with *water*. Fold dough over filling to form triangles. With a fork, crimp edges together to seal. Place on an ungreased cookie sheet.
3. Bake in a 425° oven for 8 to 10 minutes or till lightly browned. Remove from oven. Transfer tarts to wire racks. Cool. Dip tips of cooled tarts into Chocolate Glaze, if desired. Place tarts on racks till chocolate sets. Makes 24.

Chocolate Glaze: Melt together 1/2 cup *semisweet chocolate pieces* and 1 tablespoon *shortening* in small saucepan.

```
  1    cup margarine or butter
2 1/2  cups all-purpose flour
  2    cups sugar
  2    eggs
 1/2   teaspoon lemon extract
  1    beaten egg white
 1/4   cup sugar
 1/2   teaspoon ground cinnamon
       Sliced almonds
```

1. Beat margarine or butter in a bowl with an electric mixer on medium to high speed for 30 seconds or till softened. Add *half* of the flour, the 2 cups sugar, eggs, and lemon extract. Beat till mixture is thoroughly combined, scraping the sides of the bowl occasionally. Stir in the remaining flour.

2. Divide dough in half. Wrap each portion in plastic wrap or waxed paper. Chill for 1 to 2 hours.

3. Roll dough on a lightly floured surface to 1/8-inch thickness. Cut out cookies with a 2- or 2 1/2-inch-diameter cutter. Brush tops of cookies with beaten egg white. Combine the 1/4 cup sugar and cinnamon. Sprinkle mixture onto cookies. Arrange 3 or 5 almond slices on each. Place cookies 1 inch apart on greased cookie sheets.

4. Bake in a 375° oven for 8 to 9 minutes or till edges are lightly browned. Makes 5 1/2 to 6 dozen.

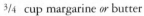

 Hermits

```
 3/4   cup margarine or butter
1 1/2  cups all-purpose flour
 3/4   cup packed brown sugar
  1    egg
 1/4   cup strong brewed coffee, cooled
  1    teaspoon ground cinnamon
 1/2   teaspoon baking soda
 1/4   teaspoon ground cloves
 1/4   teaspoon ground nutmeg
  2    cups raisins
  1    cup chopped pecans
       Pecan halves (optional)
       Sifted powdered sugar
```

1. Beat margarine or butter in a mixing bowl with an electric mixer on medium to high speed for 30 seconds. Add about *half* of the flour, the brown sugar, egg, coffee, cinnamon, soda, cloves, and nutmeg. Beat till thoroughly combined. Beat in remaining flour.

2. Stir in raisins and chopped pecans by hand. Drop by rounded tablespoons onto ungreased cookie sheet. If desired, lightly press a pecan half on each.

3. Bake in a 375° oven for 8 to 10 minutes or till edges are lightly browned. Remove; cool on wire rack. Sprinkle with powdered sugar. Makes about 48.

The taste of maple syrup, molasses, and cranberries can be found in New England cookie recipes for Mr. Joe Froggers, Maple Nut Bars, Rumprints, and Cranberry Stars.

Mr. Joe Froggers

3¹/₂ cups all-purpose flour
¹/₂ cup whole wheat flour
1¹/₂ teaspoons ground ginger
¹/₂ teaspoon baking soda
¹/₂ teaspoon ground cloves
¹/₂ teaspoon ground nutmeg
¹/₈ teaspoon ground allspice
³/₄ cup margarine *or* butter
1 cup sugar
1 cup light molasses
2 tablespoons rum *or* water
Decorator's Icing

1. Stir together all-purpose flour and whole wheat flour, ginger, baking soda, cloves, nutmeg, and allspice. In large mixer bowl beat margarine or butter 30 seconds. Add sugar; beat till fluffy. Combine molasses and rum. Add flour and molasses mixtures alternately to beaten mixture; beat well. Cover; chill several hours.

2. On a floured surface, roll dough, half at a time, to ¹/₈-inch thickness. Cut out with a 4- or 5-inch gingerbread man cookie cutter. Place on a greased baking sheet. Bake in 375° oven about 8 minutes or till set. Cool cookies 1 minute on pan. Remove to rack; cool completely. Pipe on Decorator's Icing. Makes about 40.

Decorator's Icing: Stir together 1 cup sifted *powdered sugar*, ¹/₂ teaspoon *vanilla*, and enough *light cream* or *milk* (about 1 tablespoon) to make icing of piping consistency.

2 cups fresh cranberries
1/2 cup orange marmalade
2 tablespoons honey
1/4 cup finely chopped walnuts
1 cup shortening
1/2 cup margarine *or* butter
2 cups sugar
2 eggs
1/4 cup milk
1 teaspoon vanilla
41/2 cups all-purpose flour
1 teaspoon baking soda
1/4 teaspoon salt
   Milk *or* water
   Sugar

1. In medium saucepan cook berries, marmalade, and honey, covered, till mixture boils and berries pop. Uncover; cook 5 to 10 minutes or till consistency of thick jam. Stir in nuts; cool to room temperature.

2. In large mixer bowl beat shortening and margarine 30 seconds. Add sugar; beat till fluffy. Add eggs, milk, and vanilla; beat well. Combine flour, soda, and salt. Gradually add flour mixture to egg mixture; mix well. Divide into quarters. Cover; chill 3 hours.

3. On floured surface, roll 1 portion of dough to 1/8-inch thickness. Cut cookies with a 2-inch round cookie cutter. Using a small star cutter, cut star from center of half the cookies.

4. Place a scant *1 teaspoon* cranberry mixture on each plain round. Top with a cutout cookie; seal edges with fork. Brush top with milk; sprinkle with sugar. Place on ungreased cookie sheet. Bake in a 375° oven 8 to 10 minutes or till lightly browned. Repeat with remaining dough. Cool on wire rack. Makes 60.

2/3 cup margarine *or* butter
1/3 cup sugar
1 egg
1 teaspoon vanilla
1/4 teaspoon salt
13/4 cups all-purpose flour
1/4 to 1/2 teaspoon ground nutmeg
1/4 cup margarine *or* butter
1 cup sifted powdered sugar
1 tablespoon rum *or* 1 tablespoon milk and 1/4 teaspoon rum extract
   Ground nutmeg

1. In a large mixer bowl beat the 2/3 cup margarine or butter till softened. Add sugar and beat till fluffy. Add egg, vanilla, and salt; beat well. Add flour and the 1/4 to 1/2 teaspoon nutmeg; beat till well mixed. Cover and chill 1 hour.

2. Shape into 1-inch balls. Place 2 inches apart on ungreased cookie sheet. Press down centers with thumb. Bake in 350° oven about 12 minutes or till done. Remove; cool on rack.

3. For filling, in small mixer bowl beat the 1/4 cup margarine or butter till softened. Add powdered sugar; beat till fluffy. Add rum and beat well. Pipe or spoon about *1/2 teaspoon* filling into center of each cookie. Sprinkle with nutmeg. Chill till firm. Makes 36.

Maple Nut Bars

1½ cups all-purpose flour
2 tablespoons brown sugar
½ cup margarine *or* butter
2 eggs
½ cup packed brown sugar
½ cup chopped walnuts
½ cup maple-flavored syrup
2 tablespoons margarine *or* butter, melted
1 teaspoon vanilla

1. Stir together flour and the 2 tablespoons brown sugar; cut in ½ cup margarine or butter till crumbly. Pat mixture into ungreased 11x7½x2-inch baking pan. Bake in 350° oven for 15 minutes.
2. Meanwhile, beat eggs slightly; stir in the ½ cup brown sugar, walnuts, maple syrup, melted margarine, and vanilla. Pour over baked layer.
3. Bake in a 350° oven for 25 minutes or till set. Cool slightly; cut into bars. Makes 32.

Viennese Raspberry Squares

2 egg whites
⅓ cup margarine *or* butter
1 cup all-purpose flour
⅓ cup sugar
2 egg yolks
¼ teaspoon cream of tartar
⅔ cup sifted powdered sugar
1 cup finely chopped toasted almonds *or* walnuts
⅓ cup red raspberry, peach, *or* apricot preserves

1. Place egg whites in a medium mixing bowl and let stand at room temperature for 30 minutes.
2. For crust, in another medium mixing bowl beat margarine or butter with an electric mixer on medium to high speed about 30 seconds or till softened. Add about *half* of the flour, the sugar, and egg yolks. Beat on medium to high speed till thoroughly combined, scraping sides of bowl often. Stir in remaining flour. Press mixture into an ungreased 9x9x2-inch baking pan. Bake in a 350° oven for 15 minutes.
3. Meanwhile, thoroughly wash and dry the beaters. For meringue topping, add cream of tartar to the egg whites. Beat on medium speed till soft peaks form (tips curl). Gradually add powdered sugar, beating till stiff peaks form (tips stand straight). Gently fold in nuts. Set meringue topping aside.
4. Spread preserves over top of the *hot* baked crust. Carefully spread meringue topping over the preserves layer. Bake in the 350° oven about 20 minutes more or till top is golden. Cool in pan on a wire rack. Cut into squares. Store, covered, in the refrigerator. Makes 36.

*Roly-Poly Santas are made
with balls of cookie dough
assembled on the
cookie sheet.*

Roly-Poly Santas

  1   cup margarine *or* butter
¹/2   cup sugar
  1   tablespoon milk
  1   teaspoon vanilla
2¹/4 cups all-purpose flour
      Red paste food coloring
      Miniature semisweet chocolate pieces
      Snow Frosting

1. Beat margarine or butter in a large mixer bowl till softened. Add sugar and beat till fluffy. Beat in milk and vanilla. Add flour and beat till well mixed. Remove *1 cup* of dough. Stir red paste food coloring into remaining dough till desired color is attained.

2. Shape each Santa by making *one* ³/4-inch ball and *four* ¹/4-inch balls from white dough. From red dough, shape *one* 1-inch ball and *five* ¹/2-inch balls. On ungreased cookie sheet flatten the 1-inch red ball to ¹/2 inch for body. Attach white ³/4-inch ball for head; flatten to ¹/2 inch. Attach *four* of the ¹/2-inch red balls for arms and legs. Shape remaining ¹/2-inch red ball into a hat. Place white ¹/4-inch balls at ends of arms and legs for hands and feet. Use miniature chocolate pieces for eyes and buttons.

3. Bake in a 325° oven for 12 to 15 minutes or till edges are lightly browned. Cool 2 minutes on cookie sheet. Carefully remove and cool on wire rack.

4. Prepare Snow Frosting. With a pastry tube and plain tip, pipe a band of icing on hat, cuffs at hands and feet, down the front, and at the bottom of jacket. Use a star tip to pipe beard and pom-pom on hat. Makes 12.

   Snow Frosting: In a large mixer bowl beat ¹/2 cup *shortening* and ¹/2 teaspoon *vanilla* for 30 seconds. Gradually beat in 1¹/3 cups sifted *powdered sugar*. Add 1 tablespoon *milk*. Gradually beat in 1 cup more sifted *powdered sugar* and enough *milk* (3 to 4 tablespoons) to make frosting of piping consistency.

All-Fruit Mincemeat

Make your own All-Fruit Mincemeat to use in the following cookies as well as your other holiday recipes.

4 cups chopped unpeeled apples
2 cups raisins, chopped
1 cup snipped dried apricots
1 can (6 ounces; 3/4 cup) frozen apple juice concentrate, thawed
3/4 cup water
1/4 cup honey
1 teaspoon ground allspice
1/2 teaspoon salt
2 tablespoons brandy

1. In a 4¹/2-quart Dutch oven stir together apples, raisins, apricots, apple juice concentrate, water, honey, allspice, and salt. Bring to boiling; reduce heat. Cover; simmer for 50 minutes, stirring occasionally. Uncover; simmer for 10 to 15 minutes more or till liquid has nearly evaporated, stirring occasionally. Stir in brandy. Store, covered, in refrigerator. Makes about 8 cups.

Mincemeat Drop Cookies

1 cup margarine *or* butter
3 cups all-purpose flour
1 cup sugar
2 eggs
1 teaspoon baking powder
1/4 teaspoon baking soda
2 cups All-Fruit Mincemeat or prepared mincemeat
1/2 cup chopped walnuts
Brandy Icing

1. In a bowl beat margarine 30 seconds or till softened. Add *half* the flour, sugar, eggs, baking powder, and soda. Beat till combined. Beat in remaining flour. Stir in All-Fruit Mincemeat or prepared mincemeat and walnuts.
2. Drop by rounded teaspoonfuls onto greased cookie sheets. Bake in 350° oven 11 to 13 minutes. Cool on cookie sheet 1 minute. Remove; cool. Drizzle with Brandy Icing. Makes about 72.

   Brandy Icing: In a small bowl stir together 2 cups sifted *powdered sugar*, 1 tablespoon *brandy*, and enough *milk* (2 to 3 tablespoons) to make of drizzling consistency.

Peanut Butter Drops

1/2 cup packed brown sugar
1/2 cup chunk-style *or* creamy peanut butter
1/4 cup evaporated milk
2¹/2 cups crisp rice cereal *or* granola

1. Stir together brown sugar, peanut butter, and evaporated milk in a medium saucepan. Bring to boiling, stirring constantly, till brown sugar is dissolved and peanut butter is melted.
2. Remove from heat. Stir in crisp rice cereal or granola.
3. Drop by rounded teaspoons onto waxed paper. Cool till firm. Makes 36.

 2 cups all-purpose flour
1/2 teaspoon baking powder
1/4 teaspoon baking soda
1/2 cup shortening
 1 cup packed brown sugar
 1 egg
1/2 teaspoon vanilla
11/2 cups All-Fruit Mincemeat, drained, or 11/2 cups prepared mincemeat plus 1
       teaspoon finely shredded lemon peel *or* orange peel
1/2 cup finely chopped nuts

1. Stir together flour, baking powder, and soda. In a mixer bowl beat shortening 30 seconds. Add brown sugar; beat till fluffy. Add egg and vanilla; beat well. Add dry ingredients; beat well. Cover; chill 30 minutes.
2. For filling, stir together All-Fruit Mincemeat and nuts or prepared mincemeat, peel, and nuts.
3. Divide dough in half. On waxed paper, roll 1 portion to 12x8-inch rectangle. Spread with *half* the filling. From short side, roll up jelly-roll style, removing paper as you roll. Moisten edges; pinch to seal. Repeat with remaining dough and filling. Wrap in waxed paper; chill 4 to 24 hours.
4. Cut dough into 1/4-inch-thick slices. Place 2 inches apart on greased cookie sheet. Bake in 350° oven 8 to 10 minutes or till edges are firm and bottoms lightly browned. Cool on rack. Makes about 60.

 2 cups all-purpose flour
 1 cup whole wheat flour
 1 tablespoon baking powder
 1 teaspoon ground cinnamon
1/2 teaspoon ground nutmeg
1/2 cup margarine or butter
 3 eggs
1/2 cup milk
 2 tablespoons honey
 1 slightly beaten egg white
 2 tablespoons honey
 1 cup All Fruit Mincemeat, drained, or prepared mincemeat
1/2 cup broken walnuts
    Colored sugar (optional)

1. In a large mixing bowl combine flours, baking powder, cinnamon, nutmeg, and 1/4 teaspoon *salt*. Cut in margarine or butter till pieces are the size of small peas. Stir together eggs, milk, and 2 tablespoons honey. Add to flour mixture; stir till combined. Divide dough in half.
2. On a lightly floured surface, roll out *half* the dough to 1/8-inch thickness. Using a 4-inch tree cookie cutter, cut 18 pastry trees, rerolling dough as necessary. Place on lightly greased cookie sheet.
3. Combine egg white and remaining 2 tablespoons honey. Brush trees with mixture. Combine All-Fruit Mincemeat or prepared mincemeat and walnut pieces. Place *1 rounded tablespoon* filling in center of each tree.
4. Roll and cut remaining dough as before. Place remaining trees over filling. Seal edges with tines of fork. Brush egg-white mixture over each. Sprinkle with colored sugar, if desired.
5. Bake in 375° oven for 10 to 12 minutes or till light brown. Makes 18.

Irma's Frosted Eggnog Logs

3 cups all-purpose flour
1 teaspoon ground nutmeg
1 cup margarine *or* butter
3/4 cup sugar
1 egg
2 teaspoons vanilla
1 teaspoon rum flavoring
Rum Frosting

1. Stir together the flour and nutmeg in a mixing bowl.

2. Beat margarine or butter in a large mixer bowl for 30 seconds. Add sugar and beat till fluffy. Beat in egg, vanilla, and rum flavoring till combined. Add dry ingredients and beat well.

3. Shape dough into 3-inch-long logs, about 1/2 inch wide. Arrange logs on ungreased cookie sheets.

4. Bake in a 350° oven for 15 to 17 minutes or till golden. Remove from oven and cool on wire racks.

5. Meanwhile, prepare the Rum Frosting. Spread over tops of cooled cookies. Mark the frosting lengthwise with tines of a fork to resemble bark. Sprinkle frosting with additional nutmeg. Makes about 54.

Rum Frosting: In a mixer bowl beat together 3 tablespoons softened *margarine* or *butter*, 1/2 teaspoon *rum flavoring*, and 1/2 teaspoon *vanilla*. Beat in 1/2 cup sifted *powdered sugar*. Gradually add more sifted *powdered sugar* (about 2 cups) and 2 to 3 tablespoons *evaporated milk*, *cream*, or *milk*, beating till the frosting spreads easily. Tint frosting with food coloring, if desired.

THE SEASON

Peppermint and eggnog are Christmas flavors. Ruth's Peppermint Pinwheels and Irma's Frosted Eggnog Logs capture the spirit of the season.

2¹/₂ cups all-purpose flour
 ¹/₄ teaspoon salt
   1 cup margarine *or* butter
   1 cup sifted powdered sugar
   1 egg
   1 teaspoon vanilla
   1 teaspoon almond extract *or* ³/₄ teaspoon peppermint extract
 ¹/₂ teaspoon red food coloring
   1 egg white
   1 tablespoon water
 ¹/₂ cup finely crushed peppermint candy

1. Stir together the flour and salt.
2. Beat margarine or butter in a mixer bowl for 30 seconds. Beat in powdered sugar till fluffy. Add egg, vanilla, and extract; beat well. Add the dry ingredients. Beat till just combined.
3. Divide dough in half. Mix food coloring into one portion of dough. Chill dough 1 hour or till easy to handle.
4. Divide each portion of dough in half. On lightly floured surface roll out each of the four balls of dough to form an 8-inch square.
5. Place a white square of cookie dough on top of a red square of cookie dough. Roll up, jelly-roll style. Repeat with remaining dough. Wrap the rolls in waxed paper and chill 2 to 24 hours.
6. Cut dough into ¹/₄-inch-thick slices. Place on ungreased cookie sheets. Bake in a 375° oven for 8 to 10 minutes or till edges are firm and bottoms are light brown. Remove cookies and cool on wire racks.
7. Beat together egg white and water; brush over warm cookies. Sprinkle with the crushed peppermint candy. Makes about 60.

Ruth's Peppermint Pinwheels

2¹/₄ cups all-purpose flour
   1 teaspoon baking powder
 ¹/₄ teaspoon salt
 ³/₄ cup margarine *or* butter
 ¹/₂ cup sugar
   1 egg
   2 teaspoons grated orange peel
 ¹/₂ teaspoon almond extract
     Colored sugar *or* decorative candies (optional)

1. Stir together the flour, baking powder, and salt. Set aside.
2. Beat margarine in mixer bowl for 30 seconds. Add sugar; beat till fluffy. Beat in egg, orange peel, and almond extract.
3. Add dry ingredients to mixture and beat till combined. Do not chill dough.
4. Pack dough into a cookie press. Force dough through press onto an ungreased cookie sheet. Decorate with colored sugar or candies, if desired.
5. Bake in a 400° oven for 6 to 8 minutes or till done. Remove and cool on wire racks. Makes 48.

Orange Spritz Cookies

Sugarplum Candies

Visions of sweets dance through holiday plans. Schedule candy-making time. Candy is the perfect treat to pass among friends who drop by, to pack in tins for gifts, and to enjoy with your family. Shopping experiences are forgettable, but making, sharing, and savoring homemade candy creates sweet memories.

1 package (4 ounces) sweet baking chocolate
20 chocolate sandwich cookies, finely crushed (2 cups)
1 cup toasted ground hazelnuts *or* almonds
3 tablespoons whipping cream
1 tablespoon orange liqueur *or* orange juice
1 tablespoon finely shredded orange peel
1 tablespoon orange juice *or* water
1/3 cup presweetened cocoa power or powdered sugar *or* 1/3 cup
    chocolate-flavor sprinkles or finely ground nuts

1. Melt chocolate in a heavy medium saucepan over low heat. Remove from heat and stir in crushed cookies, hazelnuts or almonds, whipping cream, orange liqueur or orange juice, orange peel, and orange juice or water. Cover and chill 1 hour or till mixture is easy to handle.
2. Shape into 1-inch balls. Roll truffles in cocoa powder, powdered sugar, chocolate-flavor sprinkles, or nuts. Store in refrigerator. Makes about 3 dozen.

   Note: You may need to roll truffles in powdered sugar and presweetened cocoa a few times before serving (truffles soak up these coatings).

Orange Truffles

EASY & ELEGANT

You decide if you want to reveal the secret of Orange Truffles (photo, left). No one will ever guess that they are so simple to make.

Orange Gumdrops

1 cup sugar
1 cup light corn syrup
3/4 cup water
1 package (1 3/4 ounces) powdered fruit pectin
1/2 teaspoon baking soda
1 1/2 teaspoons orange extract
1 teaspoon finely shredded orange peel
4 drops yellow food coloring
1 drop red food coloring
  Sugar

1. Line a 9x5x3-inch loaf pan with foil, extending foil over edges of pan. Butter the foil; set pan aside.

2. Butter the sides of a heavy 1 1/2-quart saucepan. In the saucepan combine the 1 cup sugar and the corn syrup. Cook over medium-high heat to boiling, stirring constantly with a wooden spoon to dissolve sugar. This should take about 10 minutes. Avoid splashing mixture on sides of pan. Carefully clip candy thermometer to side of pan.

3. Cook over medium-high heat, stirring occasionally, till thermometer registers 280°, soft-crack stage. The mixture should boil at moderate, steady rate over entire surface. Reaching soft-crack stage should take about 10 minutes.

4. Meanwhile, in a heavy 2-quart saucepan combine water, pectin, and baking soda. (Mixture will be foamy.) Cook over high heat to boiling, stirring constantly. This should take about 2 minutes. Remove saucepan from heat; set saucepan aside.

5. When sugar mixture has reached soft-crack stage, remove the saucepan from heat; remove candy thermometer from saucepan. Return pectin mixture to high heat; cook till mixture just begins to simmer. *Gradually* pour the hot sugar mixture in a thin stream (slightly less than 1/8-inch diameter) into the boiling pectin mixture, stirring constantly. This should take 1 to 2 minutes. Cook, stirring constantly, 1 minute more.

6. Remove saucepan from heat. Stir in orange extract, orange peel, and yellow and red food colorings. Pour candy mixture into prepared pan. Let stand about 2 hours or till firm.

7. When firm, use foil to lift candy out of pan. Use a buttered knife to cut candy into about 3/4-inch squares. Roll squares in additional sugar. Store loosely covered. Makes about 72 pieces.

Cinnamon Gumdrops: Prepare Orange Gumdrops as directed above *except* substitute 3 drops *oil of cinnamon* and 7 drops *red food coloring* for the orange extract, orange peel, and yellow and red food colorings.

Mint Gumdrops: Prepare Orange Gumdrops as directed above *except* substitute 3/4 teaspoon *mint extract* and 7 drops *green food coloring* for the orange extract, orange peel, and yellow and red food colorings.

Lemon Gumdrops: Prepare Orange Gumdrops as directed above *except* substitute 1 1/2 teaspoons *lemon extract*, 1 teaspoon finely shredded *lemon peel*, and 7 drops *yellow food coloring* for the orange extract, orange peel, and yellow and red food colorings.

1¹/₂ cups sugar
1 cup packed brown sugar
¹/₃ cup light cream
¹/₃ cup milk
2 tablespoons honey
2 tablespoons butter *or* margarine
1 teaspoon vanilla
¹/₂ teaspoon finely shredded orange peel
¹/₂ cup chopped walnuts
Walnut halves (optional)

Honey-Walnut Penuche

1. Line an 8x8x2-inch baking pan with foil, extending foil over edges of pan. Butter the foil; set pan aside.
2. Butter the sides of a heavy 2-quart saucepan. In the saucepan combine the sugar, brown sugar, cream, milk, and honey. Cook over medium-high heat to boiling, stirring constantly with a wooden spoon to dissolve sugars. This should take about 5 minutes. Avoid splashing mixture on sides of pan. Carefully clip candy thermometer to side of pan.
3. Cook over medium-low heat, stirring frequently, till thermometer registers 236°, soft-ball stage. Mixture should boil at a moderate, steady rate over the entire surface. Reaching soft-ball stage should take 15 to 20 minutes.
4. Remove pan from heat. Add the 2 tablespoons butter, vanilla, and orange peel, but *do not stir*. Cool, without stirring, to 110°, about 50 minutes. Remove thermometer. Beat vigorously till just beginning to thicken; add nuts. Continue beating till very thick and just starts to lose its gloss. This should take about 10 minutes total. Turn into prepared pan. While warm, score into 1¹/₄-inch squares. If desired, press a walnut half into each square. When firm, lift candy out of pan; cut into squares. Store tightly covered. Makes about 36 pieces or about 1¹/₂ pounds.

2 cups packed dark brown sugar
1 cup buttermilk
2 tablespoons butter *or* margarine
2 cups broken or chopped pecans

Buttermilk Pralines

1. Butter the sides of a heavy 2-quart saucepan. In the saucepan combine brown sugar and buttermilk. *(Do not substitute sour milk for the buttermilk in this recipe.)* Cook over medium-high heat to boiling, stirring constantly with a wooden spoon to dissolve sugar. This should take 6 to 8 minutes. Avoid splashing mixture on sides of pan. Carefully clip candy thermometer to pan. Cook over medium-low heat, stirring occasionally, till thermometer registers 234°, soft-ball stage. Mixture should boil at a moderate, steady rate over entire surface. Reaching soft-ball stage should take 20 to 25 minutes.
2. Remove saucepan from heat. Add the 2 tablespoons butter or margarine, but *do not stir*. Cool, without stirring, to 150°. This should take about 30 minutes. Remove candy thermometer from saucepan. Immediately stir in pecans. Beat vigorously with the wooden spoon till candy is just beginning to thicken, but is still glossy. This should take 3 to 4 minutes.
3. Quickly drop the candy from a teaspoon onto a baking sheet lined with waxed paper. If the candy becomes too stiff to drop easily from the spoon, stir in a few drops of *hot water*. Store tightly covered. Makes about 36 pralines.

Easy recipes assure great results. Wrap up some fancy gifts of Apricot Macadamia Nut Bark, Rocky Road Fudge, and Toffee Caramels.

❧ Apricot-Macadamia Nut Bark ❧

¹/2 cup coarsely chopped macadamia nuts, hazelnuts (filberts), *or* almonds
 1 pound white baking pieces with cocoa butter, cut up, *or* 1 pound vanilla-flavor confectioner's coating, cut up (3 cups)
¹/3 cup finely snipped dried apricots
 2 tablespoons finely snipped dried apricots

1. To toast nuts, spread in a single layer in a shallow baking pan. Bake in a 350° oven for 7 to 9 minutes or till toasted, stirring occasionally. Cool.
2. Meanwhile, line a baking sheet with foil; set aside.
3. Heat baking pieces or confectioner's coating in a heavy 2-quart saucepan over low heat, stirring constantly till melted and smooth. Remove from heat. Stir in nuts and the ¹/3 cup dried apricots.
4. Pour mixture onto the prepared baking sheet, spreading to about a 10-inch circle. Sprinkle with the 2 tablespoons apricots, lightly pressing into mixture. Chill about 30 minutes or till firm. (Or, if using confectioner's coating, you can let stand at room temperature for several hours or till firm.)
5. Use the foil to lift candy from the baking sheet; break candy into pieces. Store candy, tightly covered, in the refrigerator. (Or, if using confectioner's coating, you can store, tightly covered, at room temperature.) Makes about 1¹/4 pounds nut bark.

2 cups packed brown sugar
1 cup sugar
1 carton (8 ounces) dairy sour cream
1/2 cup margarine *or* butter
1/2 teaspoon ground cinnamon
1/2 teaspoon grated orange peel
1/8 teaspoon ground nutmeg
3 cups semisweet chocolate pieces (18 ounces)
1 jar (7 ounces) marshmallow cream
1 teaspoon vanilla
1 3/4 cups tiny marshmallows
1 cup chopped walnuts *or* almonds
2/3 cup raisins

1. Line a 13x9x2-inch baking pan with foil extending foil over edges. Butter the foil. Set pan aside.
2. Butter sides of heavy 3-quart saucepan. In pan combine sugars, sour cream, margarine, cinnamon, orange peel, and nutmeg. Cook over medium-high heat to boiling, stirring constantly with a wooden spoon to dissolve sugar.
3. Carefully clip candy thermometer to side of pan. Cook over medium heat, stirring frequently, till thermometer registers 232°. Remove pan from heat; remove candy thermometer from pan.
4. Add chocolate pieces, marshmallow cream, and vanilla. Stir till well blended and chocolate is melted. Quickly spread about *half* of fudge mixture in prepared pan. Sprinkle with marshmallows, *half* of the nuts, and all of the raisins. Quickly top with the remaining fudge mixture. Sprinkle with remaining nuts, pressing lightly into fudge.
5. Score into small squares while fudge is warm. When firm, lift out of pan; cut into squares. Store, tightly covered, in refrigerator. Makes about 4 pounds.

12 ounces chocolate-flavor confectioner's coating, coarsely cut up
2 packages (6 ounces each) almond brickle pieces (about 2 cups)
1 package (14 ounces) vanilla caramels (approximately 48 to 50 caramels), unwrapped

1. Place confectioner's coating in a heavy small saucepan over low heat, stirring occasionally, just till melted. Remove from heat.
2. Meanwhile, place brickle pieces in a small bowl.
3. Drop caramels, one at a time, into coating; turn to coat. With a fork, lift caramel out, drawing fork across rim of pan to remove excess coating. Drop into brickle pieces, turning to coat entire caramel. Using a fork, transfer caramel to a waxed-paper-lined baking sheet. Repeat with remaining caramels.
4. Let stand about 30 minutes or till firm. *Or*, chill about 10 minutes or till firm. Store in a tightly covered container up to 7 days. Makes 48 to 50 caramels.

Spumoni Divinity

2 1/2 cups sugar
1/2 cup light corn syrup
1/2 cup water
2 egg whites
1/2 teaspoon rum flavoring
1/4 cup finely chopped red candied cherries
1/4 cup finely chopped pistachios *or* almonds
3 or 4 drops green food coloring

1. Line a 2-quart square baking dish with foil, extending foil over edges of dish. Butter the foil; set dish aside.
2. In a heavy 2-quart saucepan combine sugar, light corn syrup, and water. Cook over medium-high heat to boiling, stirring constantly with a wooden spoon to dissolve sugar. This should take 5 to 7 minutes. Avoid splashing mixture on sides of pan. Carefully clip candy thermometer to side of pan.
3. Cook over medium heat, without stirring, till thermometer registers 260°, hard-ball stage. The mixture should boil at moderate, steady rate over entire surface. Reaching hard-ball stage should take about 15 minutes.
4. Remove saucepan from heat; remove candy thermometer from saucepan. In a large mixer bowl, immediately begin to beat egg whites with a sturdy, freestanding electric mixer on medium speed till stiff peaks form (tips stand straight).
5. *Gradually* pour hot mixture in a thin stream (slightly less than 1/8-inch diameter) over egg whites, beating with the electric mixer on high speed and scraping sides of bowl occasionally. This should take about 3 minutes. (Add mixture *slowly* to ensure proper blending.)
6. Add rum flavoring. Continue beating with electric mixer on high speed, scraping sides of bowl occasionally, just till candy starts to lose its gloss. When beaters are lifted, mixture should fall in a ribbon, mound on itself and not disappear into remaining mixture. Final beating should take 5 to 6 minutes.
7. Immediately spread *one-third* of the candy into the prepared dish. Sprinkle with the chopped candied cherries. Quickly stir finely chopped pistachios or almonds and food coloring into the remaining candy. Immediately spread over cherry layer in baking dish. When candy is firm, use foil to lift it out of dish; cut into 1-inch squares. Store tightly covered. Makes 60 pieces.

Marbleized Mint Bark

1/3 cup semisweet mint-flavor chocolate pieces or semisweet chocolate pieces
1 pound vanilla-flavor candy coating, cut up
3/4 cup finely crushed candy cane *or* finely crushed striped round peppermint candies

1. Line a baking sheet with foil; set aside. In a small saucepan heat chocolate pieces over low heat, stirring constantly, till melted and smooth. Remove pan from heat.
2. Heat the candy coating in a 2-quart saucepan over low heat, stirring constantly, till melted and smooth. Remove pan from heat. Stir in crushed candies. Pour the melted coating mixture onto the prepared baking sheet.
3. Spread the coating mixture to about a 3/8-inch thickness; drizzle with the melted chocolate. Gently zigzag a narrow metal spatula through the chocolate and peppermint layers to create a swirled effect.
4. Let candy stand for several hours or till firm. (Or, chill about 30 minutes or till firm.) Use foil to lift candy from the baking sheet; carefully break candy into pieces. Store, tightly covered, for up to 2 weeks. Makes about 1 1/4 pounds.

Quick-to-make Marbleized Mint Bark (recipe, page 118) cuts time and adds flavorful shapes to your candy supply.

Orange-Coconut Brittle

 2 cups sugar
 1 cup light corn syrup
 1 teaspoon finely shredded orange peel
 1/2 cup orange juice
 2 tablespoons butter *or* margarine
 1 1/2 teaspoons baking soda, sifted
 1 cup coconut

1. Butter two large baking sheets; set baking sheets aside. Butter the sides of a heavy 3-quart saucepan. In the saucepan combine sugar, light corn syrup, shredded orange peel, orange juice, and the 2 tablespoons butter or margarine. Cook over medium-high heat to boiling, stirring constantly with a wooden spoon to dissolve sugar. This should take about 5 minutes. Avoid splashing mixture on sides of saucepan. Carefully clip the candy thermometer to side of saucepan.

2. Cook over medium-low heat, stirring frequently, till thermometer registers 295°, hard-crack stage. Mixture should boil at a moderate, steady rate over entire surface. Reaching hard-crack stage should take about 25 minutes.

3. Remove saucepan from heat; remove candy thermometer from saucepan. Quickly sprinkle the sifted baking soda over the mixture, stirring constantly. Immediately pour mixture onto prepared baking sheets; sprinkle with coconut.

4. If desired, stretch the candy by using two forks to lift and pull the candy as it cools. Pull gently to avoid tearing the candy. Cool completely. Break candy into pieces. Store tightly covered. Makes about 1 1/2 pounds.

Peanut Brittle

2 cups sugar
1 cup light corn syrup
$^1/_2$ cup water
$^1/_4$ cup butter *or* margarine
2$^1/_2$ cups raw peanuts
1$^1/_2$ teaspoons baking soda, sifted

1. Butter two large baking sheets; set baking sheets aside. Butter the sides of a heavy 3-quart saucepan. In the saucepan combine sugar, corn syrup, water, and the $^1/_4$ cup butter or margarine. Cook over medium-high heat to boiling, stirring constantly with a wooden spoon to dissolve sugar. This should take about 5 minutes. Avoid splashing mixture on sides of pan. Carefully clip candy thermometer to side of pan.

2. Cook over medium-low heat, stirring occasionally, till thermometer registers 275°, soft-crack stage. Mixture should boil at a moderate, steady rate over entire surface. Reaching soft-crack stage should take 30 to 35 minutes. Stir in nuts. Continue cooking over medium-low heat, stirring frequently, till thermometer registers 295°, hard-crack stage. Reaching hard-crack stage should take 15 to 20 minutes more.

3. Remove pan from heat; remove thermometer. Quickly sprinkle sifted baking soda over mixture, stirring constantly. Immediately pour mixture onto prepared baking sheets. If desired, stretch candy by using two forks to lift and pull candy as it cools. Pull gently to avoid tearing. Cool completely. Break candy into pieces. Store tightly covered. Makes about 2$^1/_3$ pounds.

JEWELS

The look of stained glass in sweet treats — Crystal Candies will make you shine. Classic Peanut Brittle and Orange-Coconut Brittle (recipe, page 119) make you famous, too.

2 cups sugar
1 cup light corn syrup
1/2 cup water
1/4 teaspoon desired food coloring
Few drops oil of cinnamon, oil of peppermint, *or* oil of wintergreen

1. Line an 8x8x2-inch baking pan with foil, extending foil over edges of pan. Butter the foil; set pan aside.

2. Butter the sides of a heavy 2-quart saucepan. In saucepan combine sugar, corn syrup, and water. Cook over medium-high heat to boiling, stirring constantly with a wooden spoon to dissolve sugar. This should take about 5 minutes. Avoid splashing mixture on sides of pan. Carefully clip candy thermometer to side of saucepan.

3. Cook over medium heat, stirring occasionally, till thermometer registers 290°, soft-crack stage. Mixture should boil at moderate, steady rate over the entire surface. Reaching soft-crack stage should take 20 to 25 minutes. Remove the saucepan from heat; remove candy thermometer from the saucepan.

4. Quickly stir in desired food coloring and flavoring. Immediately pour mixture into the prepared pan. Let stand 5 to 10 minutes or till a film forms over the surface of the candy.

5. Using a broad spatula or pancake turner, begin marking candy by pressing a line across surface, 1/2 inch from edge of pan. Do not break film on surface. Repeat along other three sides of pan, intersecting lines at corners to form squares. (If candy does not hold its shape, it is not cool enough to mark. Let candy stand a few more minutes and start again.)

6. Continue marking lines along all sides, 1/2 inch apart, till you reach center. Retrace previous lines, pressing the spatula deeper but not breaking film on surface. Repeat till the spatula can be pressed to bottom of pan along all lines. Cool completely. Use foil to lift the candy out of the pan; break candy into squares.

7. (Or, to make molded candies, oil molds made for hard candies. Pour mixture into molds. Cool 10 minutes or till firm. Invert; twist molds till candies come out. Cool completely; decorate candies with Powered Sugar Icing, if desired.) Store tightly covered. Makes about 1 1/2 pounds.

Powdered Sugar Icing: Combine 1 cup sifted *powdered sugar*, 1/4 teaspoon *vanilla*, and enough *milk* (about 4 teaspoons) to make of spreading consistency.

Crystal
Candies

3/4 cup semisweet chocolate pieces
16 paper candy cups (1 1/2-inch size)
1 1/4 cups tiny marshmallows
2 tablespoons green crème de menthe
1 tablespoon white crème de cacao
1/2 cup whipping cream
Chocolate curls

1. Place chocolate pieces in a small heavy saucepan over low heat; stir constantly till chocolate is almost melted. Remove from heat and stir till smooth. With a small paintbrush, brush chocolate onto bottom and up sides of paper candy cups till chocolate is 1/8 inch thick. Wipe off any chocolate that runs over top. Chill till firm. Pull paper cups away. Store in the refrigerator.

2. In a small saucepan combine marshmallows and liqueurs. Cook over low heat till marshmallows melt, stirring occasionally. Remove from heat. Cool 10 minutes, stirring frequently.

3. In a bowl beat cream till soft peaks form. Fold in marshmallow mixture. Spoon into chocolate cups. Top with chocolate curls. Chill 4 hours or freeze. Serve chilled or frozen. Makes 16.

Grasshopper
Cups

Holiday Breads

The aroma drifting through the house, the nostalgia involved in remembering Christmases past, and the unmatched taste of homemade breads are compelling reasons to bake. Both yeast breads and quick breads are delightful additions to holiday food plans.

Cranberry-Pumpkin Bread

4 cups all-purpose flour
2 tablespoons baking powder
2 teaspoons ground cinnamon
1/2 teaspoon baking soda
1/2 teaspoon ground nutmeg
1/4 teaspoon ground ginger
2 cups sugar
2 cups canned pumpkin
1 cup frozen egg product, thawed (equivalent to 4 large eggs)
1/2 cup cooking oil
2 cups coarsely chopped cranberries
1/2 cup chopped toasted almonds
Vanilla Icing (optional)

1. Grease two 9x5x3-inch loaf pans; set aside. In a medium bowl stir together flour, baking powder, cinnamon, baking soda, nutmeg, and ginger; set aside. In a large bowl combine sugar, pumpkin, egg product, and oil. Add flour mixture to pumpkin mixture; stir just till moistened. Fold in berries and almonds.
2. Pour batter into the prepared pans. Bake in a 350° oven for 60 to 65 minutes or till a wooden toothpick inserted near the centers comes out clean.
3. Cool for 10 minutes. Remove from pans; cool. Wrap and store overnight. If desired, before serving, drizzle with Vanilla Icing. Makes 2 loaves (36 servings total).

Vanilla Icing: In a small bowl stir together 1/2 cup sifted *powdered sugar* and 1/2 teaspoon *vanilla*. Stir in enough *milk* (1 to 2 teaspoons) to make an icing of drizzling consistency. Makes about 1 cup.

HOLIDAY FARE

The flavors of the season are combined in Cranberry-Pumpkin Bread (photo, left) for coffee time or any time.

123

Cheddar Cheese Bows

6³/4 to 7¹/4 cups all-purpose flour
3 cups shredded cheddar, Swiss, *or* Monterey Jack cheese
2 packages quick-rising active dry yeast
2¹/2 cups milk
¹/2 cup sugar
1 teaspoon salt
2 eggs
Milk
Grated Parmesan cheese

1. Stir together *3 cups* of the flour, the shredded cheese, and yeast in a large mixing bowl. Set aside.
2. Combine the 2¹/2 cups milk, the sugar, and salt in a medium saucepan. Heat and stir just till warm (120° to 130°). Add to flour mixture. Add eggs.
3. Beat with an electric mixer on low to medium speed for 30 seconds, scraping sides of bowl constantly. Beat on high speed for 3 minutes. Using a spoon, stir in as much remaining flour as you can. Turn dough out onto a lightly floured surface.
4. Knead in enough of the remaining flour to make a moderately stiff dough that is smooth and elastic (6 to 8 minutes total). Shape into a ball. Place in a lightly greased bowl; turn to grease surface. Cover; let rest 10 minutes.
5. Divide dough into four portions. On a lightly floured surface, roll *one portion* into a 12-inch square. Cut square into twelve 12x1-inch strips. On a lightly greased or foil-lined baking sheet, shape each strip into a bow by forming two loops and bringing ends to center, so ends overlap about 1¹/2 inches. Holding the ends, twist together once. Press dough together at center. Cover and let rise in a warm place till nearly double (20 to 30 minutes). Repeat with remaining dough.
6. Brush rolls with additional milk; sprinkle with Parmesan cheese. Bake in a 375° oven 12 minutes or till golden. Cool on wire racks. Makes 48.

Cranberry-Apple Muffins

¹/2 cup whole cranberry sauce
¹/2 teaspoon shredded orange peel
1¹/2 cups all-purpose flour
¹/2 cup granulated sugar
1 teaspoon ground cinnamon
¹/2 teaspoon baking soda
¹/4 teaspoon baking powder
¹/4 teaspoon salt
1 slightly beaten egg
1 cup shredded peeled apple
¹/3 cup milk
¹/3 cup cooking oil
¹/2 cup sifted powdered sugar
2 to 3 teaspoons orange juice

1. Combine cranberry sauce and peel. Set aside.
2. Combine flour, sugar, cinnamon, baking soda, baking powder, and salt. Make a well in center. Combine egg, apple, milk, and oil. Add egg mixture all at once to dry ingredients. Stir just till moistened. Fill greased 2¹/2-inch muffin cups half full.
3. Make a well in center of each with back of spoon. Spoon *2 teaspoons* of cranberry mixture into each well. Bake in a 375° oven 18 to 20 minutes.
4. Combine powdered sugar and orange juice to make of drizzling consistency. Drizzle over warm muffins. Makes 12.

3¹/2 to 4 cups all-purpose flour
2 packages active dry yeast
¹/2 teaspoon ground nutmeg
1 cup canned or dairy eggnog
¹/4 cup water
¹/4 cup margarine *or* butter
¹/4 cup granulated sugar
1 teaspoon salt
1 egg
³/4 cup chopped, mixed candied fruits and peels
¹/2 cup light raisins
1 cup sifted powdered sugar
1 to 2 tablespoons canned or dairy eggnog
Candied fruit (optional)

1. Combine *1¹/2 cups* of the flour, yeast, and nutmeg in a large bowl; set aside. In a saucepan heat and stir the 1 cup eggnog, water, margarine, granulated sugar, and salt just till warm (120° to 130°) and margarine is almost melted. Add to flour mixture. Add egg. Beat with an electric mixer on low to medium speed for 30 seconds, scraping bowl. Beat on high speed for 3 minutes. Stir in fruits and peels, raisins, and as much of the remaining flour as you can.
2. Knead in enough of the remaining flour to make a moderately stiff dough that is smooth and elastic (6 to 8 minutes total). Shape into a ball. Place in a greased bowl; turn once. Cover; let rise in a warm place till double (about 1¹/2 hours).
3. Punch dough down. Turn out onto a lightly floured surface. Divide dough into three equal pieces. Cover and let rest 10 minutes. Roll each piece of dough into an evenly thick 18-inch rope.
4. To make braid, line up the three ropes, 1 inch apart, on a large greased baking sheet. Starting in the middle, loosely braid toward each end. Press ends together to seal; tuck ends under. Cover and let rise till nearly double (about 45 to 60 minutes). Bake in a 350° oven 10 minutes. Cover loosely with foil and bake 15 to 20 minutes more or till bread tests done. Cool.
5. Combine powdered sugar with enough eggnog to make a glaze of drizzling consistency. Drizzle over loaf. Garnish the top with additional candied fruit, if desired. Makes 1 braid.

2 cups all-purpose flour
1 tablespoon baking powder
¹/2 teaspoon baking soda
¹/2 cup margarine *or* butter
2 tablespoons brown sugar
1 cup dairy sour cream
¹/2 cup light molasses
2 eggs
3 cups bran cereal with raisins

1. Grease muffin cups and top of pan or spray with nonstick spray coating; set aside.
2. In a large mixing bowl mix flour, baking powder, and soda; set aside.
3. In a large mixer bowl beat margarine 30 seconds. Add brown sugar; beat till fluffy. Beat in sour cream and molasses till blended. Beat in eggs. Stir flour mixture into creamed mixture till moistened. Fold in cereal. Fill prepared muffin cups even with the top of the pan. Bake in a 350° oven about 25 minutes or till done. Remove from pan; serve warm. Makes 12.

Cherry-Almond Coffee Bread appears to have a professional touch. Wake up the people in your house with this holiday breakfast treat.

Cherry- Almond Coffee Bread

3^1/$_2$ to 4 cups all-purpose flour
1 package quick-rising active dry yeast
1 cup milk
^{1}/$_3$ cup margarine *or* butter
^{1}/$_4$ cup sugar
1 egg
^{2}/$_3$ cup cherry preserves
3 tablespoons margarine *or* butter, softened
3 tablespoons chopped almonds
Confectioner's Icing
2 tablespoons toasted sliced almonds

1. Stir together *1^1/$_2$ cups* of the flour and the yeast in a large mixer bowl. In a medium saucepan heat milk, ^{1}/$_3$ cup margarine or butter, sugar, and ^{1}/$_2$ teaspoon *salt* till warm (120° to 130°) and margarine almost melts, stirring constantly. Add to flour mixture; add egg. Beat with electric mixer on low speed 30 seconds, scraping sides of bowl constantly. Beat with mixer on high speed 3 minutes. Using a spoon, stir in as much remaining flour as you can.
2. Turn dough out onto a lightly floured surface; knead in enough remaining flour to make a moderately stiff dough that is smooth and elastic (5 to 8 minutes total). Divide dough in half; shape into two balls. Cover and let rest 10 minutes. On lightly floured surface roll one portion of dough into 16x8-inch rectangle.
3. Combine preserves, 3 tablespoons margarine, and chopped almonds. Spread dough with *half* the mixture. Roll up jelly-roll style, beginning with a long side. Seal edge. Using a sharp knife, cut the roll of dough in half lengthwise.
4. Beginning in the center of a greased 9x1^1/$_2$-inch round baking pan, loosely coil one strip of dough, cut side up. Loosely coil second strip of dough around first strip. In another pan, repeat with remaining dough and remaining cherry mixture.
5. Cover and let rise in a warm place till double (20 to 30 minutes).
6. Bake in a 350° oven about 30 minutes or till lightly browned. (If necessary, cover loosely with foil the last 10 to 15 minutes to prevent overbrowning.) Cool on wire rack. Drizzle each bread with Confectioner's Icing; sprinkle with sliced almonds. Makes 2 coffee breads.

Confectioner's Icing: In a small bowl beat 1 cup sifted *powdered sugar*, 1 tablespoon *margarine* or *butter*, and ^{1}/$_4$ teaspoon *vanilla* till combined. Beat in enough *milk* (about 3 teaspoons) to make of drizzling consistency.

  5   to 5¹/2 cups all-purpose flour
  2   packages active dry yeast
1¹/3   cups milk
 ¹/2   cup sugar
 ¹/2   cup margarine *or* butter
 ¹/2   teaspoon salt
  2   eggs
  1   cup coarsely chopped walnuts, toasted
 ¹/4   cup margarine *or* butter, melted
 ²/3   cup packed brown sugar
 ¹/2   cup whipping cream
 ¹/2   cup Kahlua *or* coffee-flavored liqueur

1. In a large mixer bowl stir together *2¹/2 cups* of flour and the yeast. In a small saucepan heat and stir milk, ¹/2 cup sugar, ¹/2 cup margarine, and salt just till warm (120° to 130°) and margarine almost melts. Add to flour mixture along with eggs. Beat with electric mixer on low speed 30 seconds, scraping sides of bowl. Beat on high speed 3 minutes. Using a wooden spoon, stir in as much remaining flour as you can.
2. Turn out onto lightly floured surface. Knead in enough remaining flour to make a moderately stiff dough that is smooth and elastic (6 to 8 minutes). Shape into a ball. Place in a lightly greased bowl; turn once. Cover and let rise in a warm place till double (about 1 hour).
3. Divide dough into thirds. Cover and let rest 10 minutes. Sprinkle *one-third* of the nuts in each of 3 greased 9x1¹/2- or 8x1¹/2-inch round baking pans. On a lightly floured surface, roll 1 portion of dough into a 10x8-inch rectangle. Spread with *one-third* of the melted margarine. Sprinkle with *one-third* of the brown sugar. Roll up, starting from one of the long sides. Seal edges. Cut into 1-inch slices. Repeat with remaining dough, margarine, and brown sugar. Place rolls, cut side down, in prepared pans. Cover and let rise till nearly double (about 30 minutes).
4. Combine the whipping cream and Kahlua. Pour ¹/3 cup of cream mixture over each pan of rolls. Bake in 375° oven for 20 to 25 minutes. Cool slightly; invert onto a serving plate. Serve warm. Makes 30 rolls.

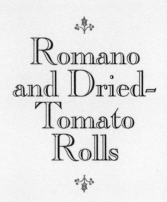

 ¹/4   cup snipped, oil-pack dried tomatoes, drained
 ¹/4   cup grated Romano cheese
  2   tablespoons pine nuts, toasted and chopped
  1   package (8) refrigerated breadsticks

1. Place dried tomatoes in a small bowl; add enough hot *water* to cover. Let stand for 10 minutes to soften. Drain. Stir in *2 tablespoons* of the cheese and pine nuts.
2. Unroll breadsticks without separating. Spread dried tomato mixture over dough. Roll dough back up. Slice where perforated. Place coils in a greased 9x1¹/2-inch round baking pan. Sprinkle with the remaining cheese.
3. Bake in a 375° oven for 18 to 20 minutes or till golden. Remove from pan. Cool thoroughly on a wire rack. Wrap in heavy foil; refrigerate for up to 3 days.
4. To serve, heat in a 325° oven for 10 to 12 minutes. Makes 8 rolls.

Christmas Bread Tree and Wreath

5 to 5¹/₂ cups all-purpose flour
2 packages active dry yeast
1¹/₄ cups milk
¹/₂ cup sugar
¹/₂ cup margarine *or* butter
¹/₂ teaspoon salt
2 eggs
1 teaspoon finely shredded lemon peel

1. In a large bowl stir together *2 cups* of the flour and the yeast. Set aside.

2. In a medium saucepan heat and stir milk, sugar, margarine or butter, and salt till warm (120° to 130°) and margarine is almost melted. Add milk mixture to flour mixture; add eggs and lemon peel. Beat on low speed for 30 seconds, scraping bowl. Beat on high speed for 3 minutes. Using a spoon, stir in as much remaining flour as you can.

3. Turn dough out onto a lightly floured surface. Knead in enough of the remaining flour to make a moderately stiff dough that is smooth and elastic (6 to 8 minutes total). Shape into a ball. Place in a lightly greased bowl; turn once to grease surface. Cover and let rise in a warm place till double (about 60 minutes). (Or, cover and let rise in the refrigerator overnight.)

4. Punch dough down. Turn out onto a lightly floured surface. Divide into 4 portions. Cover; let rest for 10 minutes. Shape and bake into desired shapes below.

Poinsettia Wreath: In a small bowl soak ²/₃ cup diced *mixed candied fruit and peels* in enough boiling *water* to cover for 5 minutes. Drain. Cut up big pieces.

Combine *2 portions* of the dough. On a lightly floured surface, roll dough to a 16x12-inch rectangle (about ¹/₄ inch thick). Brush with 3 tablespoons melted *margarine* or *butter*. Drain fruit; sprinkle over dough. Sprinkle with 3 tablespoons *sugar*. From one of the short sides, roll up jelly-roll style; seal edges. Cut diagonally into eight or nine 1-inch-thick slices plus the 2 ends.

On a greased baking sheet arrange slices, cut side down, in a 9-inch circle, overlapping edges. Place ends in center. Cover; let rise till double (30 minutes).

Sprinkle the top with *coarse sugar*, if desired. Bake in a 350° oven for 15 minutes. Cover edge with foil, leaving center uncovered. Bake about 10 minutes more or till center rolls are golden. Transfer to a wire rack to cool. Makes 1 cake (24 servings).

Sugar Plum Tree: Divide *1 portion* of dough into 4 equal parts. On a lightly floured surface, roll each part into a long ¹/₂-inch-thick rope. Transfer to waxed paper. Brush with 3 tablespoons melted *margarine* or *butter*. Combine ¹/₄ cup *sugar* and 1 teaspoon finely shredded *orange peel*; spread evenly onto paper. Roll each rope in orange peel mixture. Twist each strand.

To make a tree, on a slightly greased baking sheet, starting at the top of the tree, zigzag dough strand back and forth into wider and wider lengths. When you reach the end of one piece, attach another and continue the zigzag, ending with a curl to shape the trunk. Sprinkle with any leftover sugar-orange-peel mixture. Cover; let rise in a warm place till almost double (about 30 minutes).

Bake in a 350° oven for 15 minutes. Cover with foil and bake for 10 minutes more. Transfer to a wire rack to cool. Decorate with Orange Icing and *candied cherry halves*. Makes 1 coffee cake (12 servings).

Orange Icing: Combine 1 cup sifted *powdered sugar* and 1 teaspoon *vanilla*. Stir in enough *orange juice* (2 to 3 teaspoons) to make an icing of drizzling consistency. Makes about 1 cup.

Holiday breakfasts become parties when you serve Christmas Bread Trees and Wreaths (recipe, opposite page).

Country Scones

- ¹/₂ cup dried currants
- 2 cups all-purpose flour
- 3 tablespoons brown sugar
- 2 teaspoons baking powder
- ¹/₂ teaspoon baking soda
- ¹/₃ cup margarine *or* butter
- 1 carton (8 ounces) dairy sour cream
- 1 beaten egg yolk
- 1 slightly beaten egg white
- 1 tablespoon brown sugar
- ¹/₈ teaspoon ground cinnamon

1. In small bowl pour enough *hot water* over currants to cover; let stand 5 minutes. Drain well.

2. In large mixing bowl stir together flour, 3 tablespoons brown sugar, baking powder, soda, and ¹/₂ teaspoon *salt*. Cut in margarine or butter till mixture resembles coarse crumbs. Stir in currants. Make a well in the center. In a small bowl combine sour cream and egg yolk; add all at once to crumb mixture. Using a fork, stir just till moistened.

3. On lightly floured surface, knead gently for 10 to 12 strokes. Pat or roll to ¹/₂-inch thickness. Cut with a floured 4-inch round cookie cutter. Place scones 1 inch apart on an ungreased baking sheet. Using a sharp knife, cut each scone into 4 wedges, but do not separate. Combine egg white and 1 tablespoon *water*. Brush tops with egg-white mixture. Combine 1 tablespoon brown sugar and cinnamon; sprinkle over tops. Bake in a 425° oven 12 to 15 minutes or till light brown. Transfer to wire rack; cool 5 minutes. Break apart into wedges. Serve warm. Makes 20.

Saffron Fruit Ring

1 package (6 ounces) mixed dried fruit bits
¹/4 cup apple juice
1 package (16 ounces) hot roll mix
2 tablespoons sugar
¹/8 teaspoon ground saffron
Apple Juice Icing

1. Combine fruit and apple juice in small bowl. Let stand for 5 minutes, stirring twice.
2. Prepare roll mix according to package directions, *except* add sugar and saffron along with the flour mixture. Drain fruit, if necessary; discard excess liquid. Stir fruit into the dough before kneading.
3. Form dough into 18-inch rope on lightly floured surface. Place in greased 10-inch fluted tube pan, pressing ends together. (Make sure rope is evenly thick.) Cover; let rise according to roll-mix package directions.
4. Bake in a 375° oven 20 to 25 minutes or till golden brown. Invert onto a wire rack; cool. Drizzle with Apple Juice Icing. Makes 12 servings.

   Apple Juice Icing: In a small mixing bowl stir together 1 cup sifted *powdered sugar* and 1 to 2 tablespoons *apple juice* to make an icing of drizzling consistency. Makes about ¹/3 cup.

OLD ENGLISH

The flavor is traditional English, but the shortcut method of making Saffron Fruit Ring is up-to-date.

1³/₄ cups all-purpose flour
²/₃ cup sugar
1 tablespoon finely shredded lemon peel
1¹/₂ teaspoons baking powder
1 teaspoon poppy seed
1 egg
³/₄ cup milk
¹/₄ cup cooking oil
1 tablespoon lemon juice
Lemon Icing

Lemon-Poppy Seed Bread

1. Grease bottoms of four 4¹/₂x2¹/₂x1¹/₂-inch individual loaf pans. Set aside.

2. In a large bowl combine flour, sugar, lemon peel, baking powder, poppy seed, and dash *salt*. Combine egg, milk, oil, and lemon juice. Add to flour mixture, stirring just till moistened. Pour into prepared pans.

3. Bake in 400° oven 25 to 30 minutes or till golden brown and a toothpick inserted in the center comes out clean. Cool in the pans 10 minutes. Remove from the pans; place on a wire rack over waxed paper. Cool completely.

4. Drizzle Lemon Icing over loaves. Let icing dry till firm. Makes 4 small loaves (8 slices each).

Lemon Icing: Combine 1 cup sifted *powdered sugar* and enough *lemon juice* (4 to 5 teaspoons) to make an icing of drizzling consistency.

4³/₄ cups all-purpose flour
³/₄ cup sugar
4 teaspoons baking powder
¹/₂ teaspoon salt
¹/₂ teaspoon ground nutmeg
2 beaten eggs
2³/₄ cups canned *or* dairy eggnog
¹/₂ cup cooking oil
³/₄ cup chopped pecans
³/₄ cup snipped dried apricots
Eggnog Icing

Eggnog Bread

1. Stir together flour, sugar, baking powder, salt, and nutmeg in a large mixing bowl. Combine eggs, eggnog, and oil; add to the dry ingredients, stirring just till combined. Stir in chopped pecans and snipped apricots.

2. Turn into two greased 8x4x4-inch loaf pans. Bake in 350° oven for 55 to 60 minutes or till a toothpick inserted near centers comes out clean. (Cover with foil after 40 minutes if the bread browns too quickly.)

3. Cool in pan for 10 minutes. Remove bread from pan; cool on wire rack. Wrap bread; store overnight in refrigerator. Drizzle Eggnog Icing over bread. Makes 2 loaves.

Eggnog Icing: Stir together ²/₃ cup *powdered sugar* and 2 to 3 teaspoons canned or dairy *eggnog* to make an icing of drizzling consistency.

Building For Christmas

The construction is both fun and fascinating as candies and cookies become holiday centerpieces. Begin a family tradition building some not-so-traditional scenes. The activity will create warm, wonderful memories of sticky fingers and happy times.

1 cardboard 12-inch cake circle (available at bakeries)
1 square (12 inches) of 3/4-inch-thick plastic foam
1 square (12 inches) stiff cardboard
1 horse cookie cutter (3 inches tall)
  Food coloring
  Small paintbrush
  Pastry bags (small writing, small and medium star, and small leaf or
    small rose decorating tips)
1 striped candy stick (10 inches with 1-inch diameter)
6 striped candy sticks (8 inches)
6 striped candy sticks (4 inches)
1 striped candy ball (1-inch diameter)
6 striped candy balls (1/2-inch diameter)
2 packages flat, round citrus candies
1 package large gumdrops
4 packages candy wafers (use white only)
1 package red cinnamon candies
1 package red fruit leather strips
1 jar silver dragées
1 package tiny flavor-coated gum
  Assorted small colored candies and sugars
  Carousel Sugar Cookies
  Royal Frosting

Carousel
Sugar Cookies

1¹/2 cups margarine *or* butter
   2 cups sugar
   1 egg
   4 cups all-purpose flour
 ¹/4 teaspoon baking soda

1. Beat margarine or butter in a large mixer bowl with electric mixer on medium speed for 30 seconds. Add sugar and beat till fluffy. Add egg; beat well.
2. Stir together flour and baking soda. With mixer on low speed gradually add flour mixture to margarine mixture, beating well. Stir in last cup of flour by hand, if necessary. Cover and chill about 2 hours or till firm enough to roll.
3. Make second recipe of dough. *Do not double recipe.*
4. Cut and bake as directed in assembly instructions following.

Carousel
Royal Frosting

   3 egg whites
   1 package (16 ounces) powdered sugar, sifted
   1 teaspoon vanilla
 ¹/2 teaspoon cream of tartar

1. In a large mixer bowl combine egg whites, powdered sugar, vanilla, and cream of tartar. Beat with electric mixer on high speed for 7 to 10 minutes or till the mixture is very stiff. Use at once.
2. While using the frosting, keep the bowl covered with wet paper towels at all times to prevent it from drying as you work. The frosting can be refrigerated overnight in a tightly covered container; stir before using. Makes 3 cups.

Carousel
Cutting and baking cookies

1. Enlarge the pattern pieces as directed on pages 138 and 139.
2. Divide Carousel Sugar Cookies dough into *four* portions. Using a floured rolling pin, roll *one* portion to ¹/4-inch thickness on an ungreased baking sheet or the *back* of a 15x10x1-inch baking pan. Lay pattern for base (semi-circle) on dough. Using a sharp knife, cut around pattern *(photo 1, page 136)*. Remove excess dough; reserve for rerolling. Bake in a 350° oven about 10 minutes or till edges just begin to brown. Lay pattern on hot cookie and trim straight edge. Let cookie cool 2 minutes; loosen with spatula but do not remove from pan. Cool cookie completely. Repeat with another dough portion and same pattern.
3. Roll another portion of dough ¹/4 inch thick. Lay pattern for floor (circle) on dough. Using a sharp knife, cut around pattern; cut hole in center. Remove and reserve excess dough. Bake in 350° oven about 14 minutes or till edges just begin to brown. Lay pattern on hot cookie and recut center hole. Let cookie cool 2 minutes; loosen with spatula but do not remove from pan. Cool completely.
4. On lightly floured surface, roll last portion of dough ¹/8 to ¹/4 inch thick. Cut 6 canopy sections; remove and reserve excess dough. Transfer to ungreased baking sheet. Using Egg Paint *(see page 135)* and a small brush, paint one canopy section with each color; leave 3 canopy sections unpainted. For more intense color, let Egg Paint dry 1 minute; paint again.
5. Bake in 350° oven about 9 minutes or till edges just begin to brown. Lay patterns on hot cookies and trim edges. (Paint may crack slightly during baking. Touch up cracks with Egg Paint while cookies are hot.) Remove to wire rack; cool completely.

Egg Paint: Beat together 1 *egg yolk* and 1 teaspoon *water*. Divide mixture among three bowls. Add about ⅛ teaspoon red, yellow, or green *food coloring* to each bowl; mix well.

6. Reroll the remaining dough to ⅛-inch thickness; cut 6 side panels. Using a horse-shape cookie cutter, cut 6 or 8 horses. (You'll need just 6 but it's helpful to have extras for decorating practice.) Paint 2 horses of each color, using painting procedure previously described. Bake in a 350° oven 8 to 9 minutes or till edges just begin to brown. Lay pattern on hot cookies; trim ends. Touch up cracks. Cool on wire rack.

1. Using Royal Frosting *(recipe, page 134)* in a pastry bag with a writing tip, pipe a lattice design on each colored canopy section. While frosting is soft, place silver dragées where lines cross. Using rose or leaf tip, pipe curved edge of each lattice section *(photo 2, page 136)*. Let dry.
2. Beginning at the curved edge, "shingle" unpainted canopy sections with white candy wafers, using a dab of frosting to hold each in place. Cut several wafers with a knife to fill spaces at sides. Place a red cinnamon candy between wafers, attaching with frosting. Let dry.
3. Pipe lattice design on one side panel of each color; place dragées where lines cross. Decorate remaining panels with piped frosting and small colored candy "jewels." Let dry.

1. Using hexagon pattern, cut one piece of plastic foam and one of stiff cardboard. Using a pastry bag and writing tip, pipe some frosting on cardboard circle. Center semicircle cookies on cardboard circle; press lightly. Pipe a line of frosting where cookies join; smooth with spatula.
2. Center hexagon pattern on cookie base; draw light pencil line around it. Pipe line of frosting about 1 inch inside pencil line. Place plastic foam inside pencil line; press lightly.
3. Pipe line of frosting on back and bottom edge of a side panel; press against plastic foam. Pipe line of frosting at one end. Pipe line of frosting on back and bottom edge of another panel; place next to the first. Repeat alternating colors, till all panels are in place. Using a star tip, pipe additional frosting between panels.
4. Pipe line of frosting around top of plastic foam. Place floor circle atop, lining up holes; press lightly. Smooth both ends of 10-inch candy stick by scraping carefully with a knife. Pipe frosting in and around center hole. Insert stick so it goes through plastic foam to base *(photo 3, page 136)*.
5. Using an apple corer, cut a hole in the center of each flat round citrus candy. Smooth ends of 8-inch candy sticks; insert stick in each flat candy. Using a writing tip, pipe frosting around base of stick; attach dragées, if desired. Attach sticks to floor of carousel with frosting, placing above corners where side panels meet and about ½ inch from the edge of floor. Using a star tip, pipe line of frosting around base of candy.
6. Place a dab of frosting at top of each stick. Fit cardboard hexagon over center candy stick so it rests on upright sticks. Adjust uprights, if necessary, so they are straight. Let dry 1 hour.
7. Using kitchen scissors, cut fruit leather in scallop design. Pipe frosting around edge of cardboard; press fruit leather in place.
8. Place large dollop of frosting atop center pole. Pipe frosting around outer edge of cardboard hexagon. Place the point of a canopy section on center pole, letting canopy rest against cardboard *(photo 4, page 136)*. Pipe frosting between canopy sections. Repeat with remaining sections, alternating lattice and shingled sections. Using a leaf or a rose tip, pipe frosting over seam between sections.
9. If desired, decorate 1-inch-diameter striped candy ball with frosting and dragées. Place dollop of frosting at canopy peak; put candy ball on top.

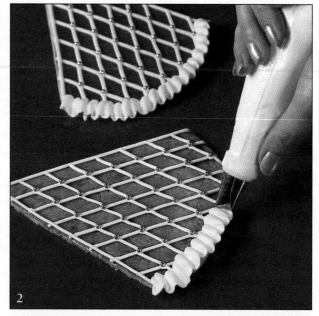

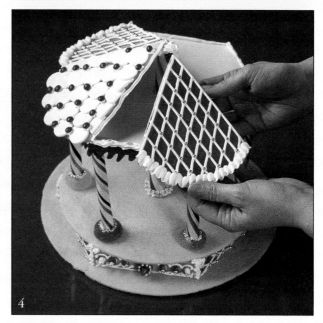

Step by step, you're building smiles.
When you supply this merry carousel for a Christmas party
centerpiece, you'll be responsible for the twinkle in the eyes of
children and grandparents and all guests who
are young at heart.

1. To decorate horses, use a pastry bag fitted with a small writing or star tip to pipe lines for bridles, saddles, manes, and tails. While frosting is soft, add dragées, colored sugar, and other small candies. Let dry.

2. Chill six large gumdrops. Using the point of an apple corer, cut an opening in top and bottom of each gumdrop *(photo 5, above)*. Level tops and bottoms of six 4-inch candy sticks. Insert a candy stick in each gumdrop; stand upright and adjust to vertical. Using a small star tip, pipe a line of stars around base of candy stick.

3. Put a dab of frosting at the top of each stick; top with 1/2-inch-diameter striped candy ball. Pipe a line of frosting around top of stick; apply dragées, if desired. Let frosting dry 1 hour.

4. Place horse face down. Pipe a band of frosting vertically on back of horse. Place candy stick in frosting; press gently *(photo 6, above)*. Let dry.

1. Place a horse on floor about 1 inch from edge between a pair of support sticks, using frosting to cement in place. Repeat with remaining horses.

2. Using a leaf or rose tip, pipe a line of frosting around the edge of the carousel base. Add additional frosting and candy embellishments, if desired.

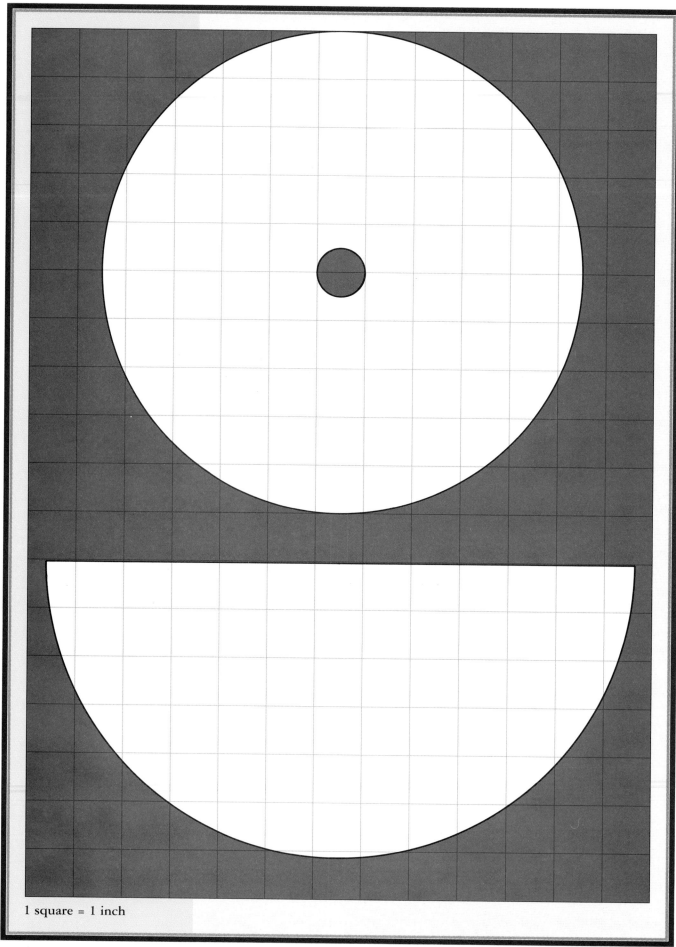

1 square = 1 inch

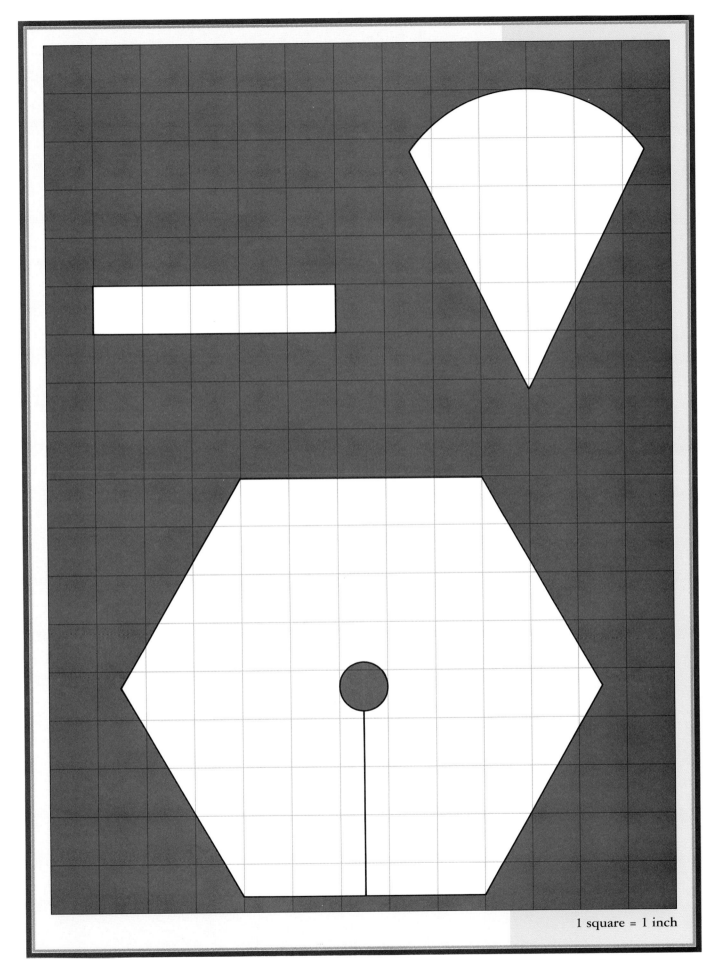

1 square = 1 inch

Farmyard
Ginger-Cookie Dough

³/4 cup margarine *or* butter
³/4 cup shortening
1¹/2 cups sugar
1 egg
³/4 cup molasses
2 tablespoons lemon juice
4¹/2 cups all-purpose flour
1¹/2 cups whole wheat flour
2 teaspoons ground ginger
2 teaspoons ground allspice
1¹/2 teaspoons baking soda
³/4 teaspoon salt

1. In a large mixer bowl beat margarine and shortening with electric mixer on medium speed till softened. Add sugar; beat till fluffy. Add egg, molasses, and lemon juice; beat till well combined.

2. Combine flours, ginger, allspice, baking soda, and salt. Gradually add to margarine mixture; beat well. Divide dough into 4 equal portions; wrap each in clear plastic wrap. Chill 3 hours or till firm enough to roll.

3. Meanwhile, enlarge pattern pieces for Gingerbread Farmyard *(page 144)*. Grease the outside bottom of a 15x10x1-inch baking pan.

COUNTRY STYLE

A barn raising involves many hands and joyful sharing. This Gingerbread Farmyard brings the spirit home.

1. Roll out one portion of the dough ¼ inch thick on the back of the prepared pan. Place enlarged patterns for barn front and side on dough. Using a sharp knife, cut around patterns. Remove excess dough; reserve for rerolling.
2. Using a table knife, cut through outlines of front barn doors; *do not remove dough*. Score lines for windows, side doors, and siding. *(See photo 1, page 143.)*
3. Bake in a 375° oven for 10 to 12 minutes. Remove gingerbread from oven. Lay patterns over cookies; trim edges if necessary. Recut the front doors. Cool on pan 1 minute. Transfer to a wire rack; cool completely.
4. Remove the doors. Repeat with additional dough and the remaining barn and roof pieces. On the roof pieces, score lines for shingles.

Farmyard — Barn

1. Repeat with additional dough and enlarged silo patterns, rolling dough ¼ inch thick. Reroll dough as necessary.
2. To form roof, shape foil into a 3-inch ball; flatten one side slightly to make into dome shape about 2 inches tall. Using a 4-inch circle of dough, press around and underneath foil dome till completely covered. Place seam side down on an ungreased baking sheet.
3. Bake in a 375° oven for 10 to 12 minutes. Remove from oven. Lay pattern over the silo panel cookies; trim edges if necessary. Let cool on the pan for 1 minute. Remove to a wire rack; cool.

Farmyard — Silo

1. On a lightly floured surface, roll dough ⅛ inch thick. Cut fence and circles for bases using enlarged patterns from page 144. Cut animals using farm-animal cutters.
2. Bake in a 375° oven 8 to 10 minutes. Transfer to wire rack; cool completely. Decorate animals as shown in photo, *opposite,* using Royal Frosting *(recipe, page 134).*

Farmyard — Fence, animals, and bases

Farmyard

Assembling farmyard

1. Cut a 14x11-inch piece of white cardboard for the base of the barnyard. Cut another piece of cardboard from the barn back pattern for a center roof support.
2. Fit pastry bag with writing tip; fill half full with Royal Frosting. Outline doors, windows, and diagonal trim.
3. Assemble barn on the cardboard base. To join barn sides to back and front pieces, using star tip, pipe frosting on edges to be joined; press together. (Small blobs of floral clay can be used to hold the corners of the barn in place till the frosting is thoroughly dry.) Insert cardboard cutout in center of barn and secure with frosting to sides of barn. *(See photo 2, opposite.)* Let frosting dry completely. Attach front doors.
4. Pipe frosting on top edges of barn and center support. Press roof pieces into place. Pipe frosting into seams between roof pieces. Outline shingles using the writing tip.
5. Decorate each silo panel top with checkerboard pattern. Cut a 6-inch length from a cardboard tube from plastic wrap or foil. With the star tip, pipe a line of frosting on center back of one silo wall; press to the cardboard tube. *(See photo 3, opposite.)* Repeat with remaining wall pieces. Pipe frosting down the edges where walls meet. Pipe frosting around the top edge of the silo; press on dome. Using the writing tip, decorate the dome as shown in photo on page 140.
6. Decorate animals; stick to half-circle bases with frosting blobs. Place between custard cups till frosting is dry. *(See photo 4, opposite.)* Arrange fence sections in zigzag line; secure to bases with frosting.

Farmyard

Hay bales

1. To make hay bales, place 1½ cups *coconut* in a covered bowl. Add several drops *green food coloring*; shake vigorously. In bowl combine 3½ cups sifted *powdered sugar*, 1 package (3 ounces) softened *cream cheese*, and 1 teaspoon *vanilla*. Stir in coconut.
2. Turn onto a piece of buttered foil. Pat to a 6x5-inch rectangle. Cut into 1½x1-inch rectangles. Tie with yellow or white string.

Farmyard

Straw

1. To make straw, tint a small amount of coconut yellow. Pipe frosting along edge of small barn door. Sprinkle coconut over frosting.

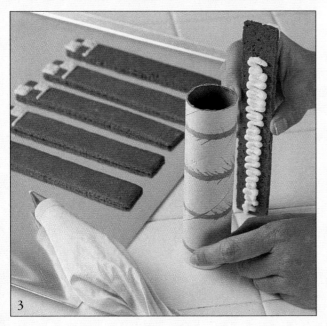

*Assemble a country-style celebration by building a barn
for your holiday table. Use the farm animals as a favor in front of
each place setting. Provide plenty of hay bales for their greenery
and the message of a feast.*

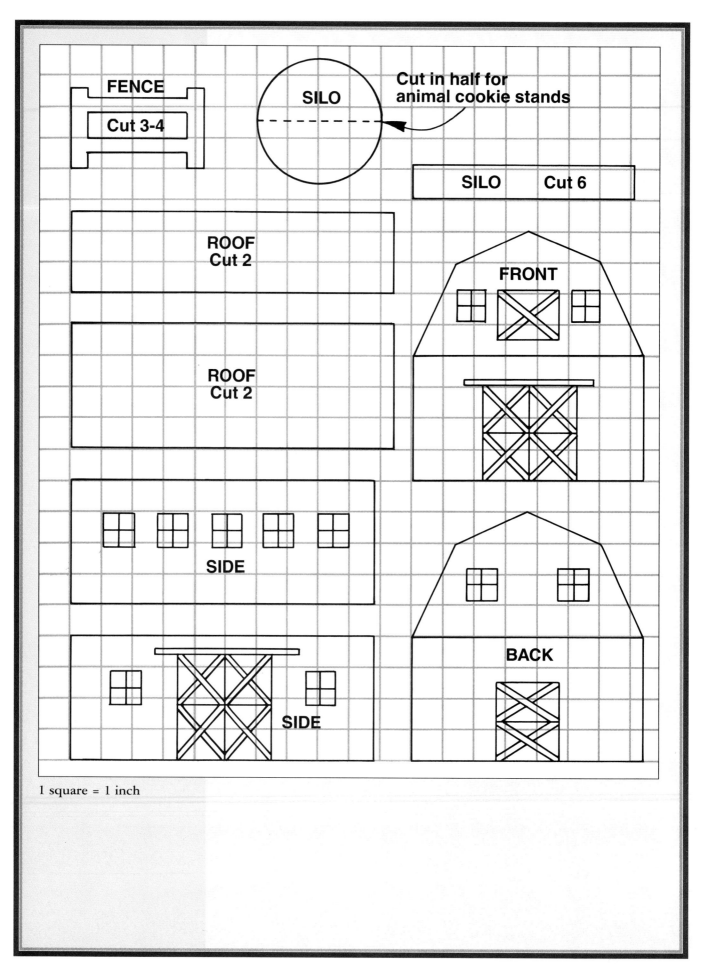

FENCE

Cut 3-4

SILO

Cut in half for animal cookie stands

SILO **Cut 6**

ROOF Cut 2

ROOF Cut 2

FRONT

SIDE

SIDE

BACK

1 square = 1 inch

    1   cup margarine *or* butter
   2/3 cup packed brown sugar
   2/3 cup corn syrup *or* molasses
    4   cups all-purpose flour
   3/4 teaspoon baking soda
    2   teaspoons ground cinnamon
    1   teaspoon ground ginger
   3/4 teaspoon ground cloves
    1   beaten egg
  1 1/2 teaspoons vanilla
        Decorating Frosting
        Miniature semisweet chocolate pieces
        Medium-size candy canes
        Graham crackers

1. Stir the margarine, brown sugar, and corn syrup in a saucepan over medium heat till margarine melts and sugar dissolves. Pour into large mixing bowl; cool 5 minutes.

2. Meanwhile, stir together flour, soda, cinnamon, ginger, and cloves. Add egg and vanilla to the margarine mixture; mix well. Add flour mixture and beat till well mixed. Cover and chill dough 2 hours or overnight.

3. To make an adult bear, shape dough into one 1 1/2-inch ball for body, one 1-inch ball for head, three 1/4-inch balls for nose and ears, two 1 3/4-inch-long by 1/2-inch-wide logs for arms, and two 1 1/2-inch-long by 3/4-inch-wide logs for legs. (For youth bears, make balls and logs a little smaller than for adult bears. For baby bears, make balls and logs a little smaller than for youth bears.)

4. Assemble heads, bodies, and arms of bears on an ungreased cookie sheet, flattening balls slightly and pressing balls and logs together. *Do not attach legs.*

5. To decorate, press in chocolate pieces, point side up, for eyes. For paws, press chocolate pieces, point side down, into ends of arms and legs. (Legs are separate from body.)

6. Bake in a 325° oven 15 minutes for adults, 12 minutes for youths, 8 minutes for babies or till edges are light brown. Transfer to a rack; cool.

7. Make sled by attaching candy-cane runners to graham cracker with Decorating Frosting. Attach body upright to sled with Decorating Frosting. Use the frosting to attach legs to body and sled as if bear were sitting. Makes 12 adult or 21 youth or 36 baby bear cookies.

Skating Teddies: Shape as directed above, *except* attach legs when assembling. For bears holding hands, assemble side by side on baking sheet. Press hands together. Decorate and bake as directed above. Cut small rectangles of heavy foil; diagonally trim ends to resemble skate blades. Attach under ends of bear's legs with Decorating Frosting, leaving the longer side of each foil "blade" showing.

Decorating Frosting: Beat 1/4 cup *shortening* and 1/4 teaspoon *vanilla* 30 seconds or till softened. Gradually beat in 1 1/4 cups *powdered sugar*. Beat in enough *milk* (about 1 tablespoon) to make of spreading consistency.

Christmas Mice

NIGHT BEFORE

*The creatures are stirring —
looking for yummy treats.
These Christmas Mice (photo,
right) are made from
cinnamony yeast dough with
almond ears, currant eyes,
and string tails.*

2¹/4 to 2³/4 cups all-purpose flour
  1 package active dry yeast
  1 teaspoon ground cinnamon
¹/2 cup milk
¹/3 cup cooking oil
  3 tablespoons sugar
  2 eggs
  2 teaspoons finely shredded orange peel
  1 slightly beaten egg white
 24 blanched almonds, split
 48 currants

1. Combine *1 cup* of flour, yeast, and cinnamon in a bowl. Heat and stir milk, oil, sugar, and ¹/4 teaspoon *salt* till warm (120° to 130°). Add to flour mixture; add eggs and orange peel. Beat with electric mixer on low speed 30 seconds, scraping bowl. Beat on high speed 3 minutes. Stir in as much remaining flour as you can. Knead in enough remaining flour to make a moderately soft dough that is smooth and elastic (3 to 5 minutes). Place in greased bowl; turn once. Cover; let rise till double (about 1¹/2 hours).
2. Punch down. Turn out onto floured surface. Cover; let rest 10 minutes. Divide into 24 portions; shape into pointed oval shapes. Place 1¹/2 inches apart on greased baking sheet. Cover; let rise till nearly double (30 to 45 minutes). Brush with egg white. Insert halved almonds for ears, currants for eyes. Bake at 375° for 10 to 12 minutes or till golden brown.
3. Cut 24 tails (3 inches each) from coarse string; tie a knot ¹/2 inch from one end of each. Make a hole in mouse with skewer; insert unknotted end. Makes 24.

Rudolph's Peanut-Butter Cookies

¹/2 cup margarine *or* butter
¹/2 cup peanut butter
1¹/4 cups all-purpose flour
¹/2 cup sugar
¹/4 cup honey
  1 egg
¹/2 teaspoon baking soda
¹/2 teaspoon baking powder
¹/2 teaspoon vanilla
³/4 cup chopped peanuts
 64 small pretzels
 32 small red gumdrops
    Semisweet chocolate pieces

1. Beat margarine or butter and peanut butter for 30 seconds. Add *half* the flour, the sugar, honey, egg, baking soda, baking powder, and vanilla. Beat till thoroughly combined. Stir in the remaining flour. Stir in peanuts. Cover and chill 1 hour or till easy to handle.
2. Work with half the dough at a time, keeping the rest refrigerated. Using *1 tablespoon* dough, shape into a triangle about 2¹/2 inches long and 2 inches wide on an ungreased cookie sheet. Lightly press pretzel antlers into sides at wide end of triangles. Add gumdrop noses and chocolate pieces for eyes.
3. Bake in a 375° oven 7 to 8 minutes or till bottoms are lightly browned. Let cool 2 minutes on cookie sheet. Carefully remove to rack to cool. Makes 32.

Giftbasket Foods

Say Merry Christmas to neighbors, friends, and relatives with packaged treats from your kitchen. Although your costs are minimal, your thoughtfulness will earn heartfelt appreciation. Foods add a personal touch when accompanying another gift. Candy, cookie, and bread recipes elsewhere in this book also make terrific gifts!

Caramel Corn and Candy Crunch

7   cups popped popcorn (about 1/3 cup unpopped)
3/4 cup packed brown sugar
1/3 cup margarine *or* butter
3   tablespoons light corn syrup
1/4 teaspoon baking soda
1/4 teaspoon vanilla
1   cup candy-coated milk chocolate pieces
1   cup peanuts
1   cup raisins

1. Remove all unpopped kernels from popped corn. Place popcorn in a greased 17x12x2-inch baking pan. Keep popcorn warm in a 300° oven while making caramel mixture.
2. Butter the sides of a heavy 1¹/₂-quart saucepan. In the saucepan combine brown sugar, margarine or butter, and corn syrup. Cook over medium heat to boiling, stirring constantly with a wooden spoon to dissolve sugar. This should take 7 to 10 minutes. Avoid splashing mixture on sides of pan. Carefully clip candy thermometer to side of pan.
3. Cook over medium heat, stirring occasionally, till thermometer registers 255°, hard-ball stage (this should take about 4 minutes). The mixture should boil at a moderate, steady rate over entire surface.
4. Remove saucepan from heat; remove candy thermometer from saucepan. Add baking soda and vanilla; stir till combined. Pour caramel mixture over the popcorn; stir gently to coat. Bake in a 300° oven for 10 minutes; stir. Bake for 5 minutes more.
5. Turn popcorn mixture onto a large piece of foil. Cool completely. Break popcorn mixture into small pieces. Stir in candy-coated chocolate pieces, nuts, and raisins. Store in a tightly covered container. Makes 9 cups.

TREATS

Pick family favorites for perfect gifts. The photo, left, features Caramel Corn and Candy Crunch and Honey-Macadamia Nut Fudge (recipe, page 150).

Honey-Macadamia Nut Fudge

1¹/₂ cups sugar
1 cup packed brown sugar
¹/₃ cup half-and-half *or* light cream
¹/₃ cup milk
2 tablespoons honey
2 tablespoons margarine *or* butter
1 teaspoon vanilla
¹/₂ cup toasted macadamia nuts, hazelnuts or pecans, chopped
Chocolate-Covered Macadamia Nuts (optional)

1. Prepare Chocolate-Covered Macadamia Nuts, if using; set aside. Line an 8x8x2-inch baking pan with foil, extending foil over edges of the pan. Butter the foil; set pan aside.
2. Butter the sides of a heavy 2-quart saucepan. In the saucepan combine the sugar, brown sugar, half-and-half or cream, milk, and honey. Bring to boiling over medium-high heat, stirring constantly with a wooden spoon to dissolve sugars. This should take about 5 minutes. Avoid splashing mixture on sides of the pan. Carefully clip candy thermometer to side of pan.
3. Cook over medium-low heat, stirring frequently, till the thermometer registers 236°, soft-ball stage (this should take 10 to 20 minutes). The mixture should boil at a moderate, steady rate over entire surface. Remove pan from heat. Add the 2 tablespoons margarine or butter and vanilla, but *do not stir*. Cool, without stirring, to 110°. This will take about 50 minutes. Remove thermometer.
4. With a wooden spoon, beat vigorously till mixture just begins to thicken; add chopped nuts. Continue beating till mixture is very thick and just starts to lose its gloss. This should take about 10 minutes total. Turn into prepared pan. While warm, score into 1¹/₄-inch squares. If desired, press 1 Chocolate-Covered Macadamia Nut into each square. When firm, lift candy out of the pan and cut into squares. Store in a tightly covered container. Makes 36 pieces (about 1¹/₂ pounds).

Chocolate-Covered Macadamia Nuts: In a small heavy saucepan melt 4 ounces *chocolate-flavored candy coating* over low heat. Remove from heat. Dip about 36 toasted *macadamia nuts*, *hazelnuts*, or *pecan halves* into coating, one at a time, covering half of each nut. Let excess coating drip off. Transfer dipped nuts to a piece of waxed paper to dry. Makes about 36 pieces.

Apple-Nutmeg Conserve

5 cups chopped peeled apples
1 cup water
¹/₃ cup lemon juice
1 package (1³/₄ ounces) powdered fruit pectin
4 cups sugar
1 cup light raisins
¹/₂ teaspoon ground nutmeg

1. Combine apples, water, and lemon juice in a 6- to 8-quart Dutch oven. Bring to boiling; reduce heat. Simmer, covered, for 10 minutes. Stir in powdered pectin and bring to a full rolling boil, stirring constantly. Stir in sugar and raisins. Return to a full rolling boil. Boil hard for 1 minute, stirring constantly. Remove from heat. Stir in nutmeg.
2. Ladle at once into hot, sterilized half-pint jars, leaving ¹/₄-inch headspace. Adjust lids. Process in boiling-water canner for 5 minutes (start timing when water boils). Makes 6 half-pints, 6 gifts.

*Delicious Banana
Gingerbread will be enjoyed
by anyone on your gift list.*

Banana Gingerbread

2¼ cups all-purpose flour
½ cup sugar
1½ to 2 teaspoons ground ginger
1 teaspoon baking powder
1 teaspoon ground cinnamon
½ teaspoon baking soda
¼ teaspoon salt
1 cup mashed ripe banana (2 to 3 medium bananas)
½ cup margarine *or* butter
½ cup molasses
3 eggs
½ cup chopped walnuts or almonds

1. Combine *1 cup* of the flour, the sugar, ginger, baking powder, cinnamon, baking soda, and salt in a large mixer bowl. Add mashed banana, margarine or butter, and molasses. Beat with an electric mixer on low speed till blended, then on high speed for 2 minutes. Add remaining flour and eggs; beat till blended. Stir in nuts.
2. Divide batter among three greased 5½x3x2-inch loaf pans. Bake in a 350° oven for 40 minutes or till a toothpick inserted near the center comes out clean. Cool in pans for 10 minutes on a wire rack. Remove from pans; cool thoroughly on wire rack.

Surprising flavors add delight to those lucky enough to receive your Marinated Cheese and Vegetables, Cajun or Basil-Garlic Bagel Chips.

Marinated Cheese and Vegetables

6 ounces provolone *or* Monterey Jack cheese
6 ounces cheddar cheese
1 can (6 ounces) pitted ripe olives, drained
1 medium sweet red pepper, seeded and cut into 1-inch squares
1 medium green pepper, seeded and cut into 1-inch squares
2 cups cauliflower flowerets
$^{1}/_{2}$ cup chopped onion
$^{2}/_{3}$ cup vinegar
$^{1}/_{2}$ cup olive oil *or* salad oil
2 tablespoons sugar
2 teaspoons dried oregano, crushed
1 teaspoon crushed red pepper
$^{1}/_{2}$ teaspoon salt

1. Cut cheeses into $^{3}/_{4}$-inch cubes. In a large bowl toss together cheeses, olives, peppers, cauliflower, and onion.
2. Combine vinegar, oil, sugar, oregano, red pepper, and salt in a screw-top jar. Cover, shake well. Pour over cheese and vegetables. Stir gently to coat. Cover and store in refrigerator overnight or up to 7 days, stirring occasionally.
3. For giving, transfer to glass jars. Enclose a card with the suggestion: *Store in refrigerator. Let stand at room temperature 30 minutes before serving.* Makes 8 cups, 6 gifts.

6 plain unsliced bagels
¹/₂ cup margarine *or* butter, melted
¹/₄ teaspoon dried thyme, crushed
¹/₄ teaspoon onion salt
¹/₈ to ¹/₄ teaspoon ground red pepper
¹/₈ teaspoon black pepper
¹/₈ teaspoon garlic powder

1. Slice each bagel vertically into ¹/₈-inch-thick slices. In a small bowl stir together melted margarine, thyme, onion salt, red pepper, black pepper, and garlic powder. Brush one side of bagel slices with margarine mixture. Arrange bagels in a single layer on baking sheets. Bake in a 400° oven 5 to 6 minutes or till top edges are crisp. Turn chips over. Bake about 4 to 5 minutes longer or till crisp. Cool on wire rack.
2. For giving, place chips in clear plastic gift boxes or bags. Makes about 60 chips, 2 gifts.
   Basil-Garlic Bagel Chips: Crush 2 cloves *garlic* in a small saucepan. Add ¹/₄ cup *olive oil* and ¹/₄ cup *margarine* or *butter*. Cook over medium heat till margarine is melted. Remove from heat; let stand 30 minutes. Remove garlic. Stir in 1 tablespoon snipped *fresh basil* or 1 teaspoon *dried basil*, crushed. Brush on bagel slices and bake as above.

¹/₂ cup Dijon-style mustard
¹/₃ cup cooking oil
¹/₄ cup white vinegar
¹/₄ cup dry white wine
2 tablespoons dry mustard
1 teaspoon dried basil, crushed
1 teaspoon dried tarragon, crushed

1. Stir together mustard, oil, vinegar, wine, dry mustard, basil, and tarragon in a small mixing bowl.
2. For giving, transfer sauce to small jars with tight-fitting lids. Include serving suggestion: *Store in refrigerator. Serve with meats or vegetables.* Makes 1¹/₃ cups, 2 gifts.

5 large tomatoes, peeled and diced (5 cups)
1 large onion, chopped (1 cup)
¹/₂ cup lemon juice
4 or 5 fresh *or* canned jalapeño peppers, seeded and finely chopped
3 tablespoons snipped fresh cilantro
4 cloves garlic, minced
2 teaspoons sugar
2 medium oranges, peeled, sectioned, and chopped

1. Combine tomatoes, onion, lemon juice, peppers, cilantro, garlic, sugar, and 1 teaspoon *salt* in a 4-quart kettle or Dutch oven. Bring mixture to boiling. Reduce heat and boil gently about 30 minutes or till mixture is desired consistency. Stir in oranges. Return to boiling.
2. Immediately ladle salsa into hot, sterilized half-pint jars, leaving ¹/₂-inch headspace. Adjust lids. Process in a boiling-water canner for 30 minutes. Makes about 4 half-pints, 4 gifts.

Black Jack Barbecue Sauce

4 to 6 fresh jalapeño chili peppers
4 medium onions, chopped
1 cup catsup
1 cup strong coffee
$2/3$ cup Worcestershire sauce
$1/2$ cup packed brown sugar
$1/2$ cup vinegar
3 tablespoons chili powder
6 cloves garlic, sliced
2 teaspoons salt

1. Wearing plastic bags on your hands, halve chili peppers; remove and discard seeds. Chop chili peppers (you should have $1/4$ cup). Combine chili peppers and remaining ingredients in a 2-quart saucepan. Bring to boiling. Reduce heat and simmer, uncovered, 25 minutes. Cool mixture slightly.
2. Blend or process the mixture, half at a time, in a blender container or food processor bowl till nearly smooth. Cool.
3. For giving, transfer sauce to four 1-cup jars with tight-fitting lids. Store in refrigerator. Makes 4 cups, 4 gifts.

Tomatillo-Apple Salsa

24 fresh tomatillos, hulled and chopped ($4^{2}/3$ cups), *or* 4 cans (18 ounces each) tomatillos, drained and chopped
3 medium tart apples, peeled, cored, and finely chopped (2 cups)
$1/2$ cup chopped sweet red pepper
$1/2$ cup cider vinegar
4 to 6 fresh *or* canned jalapeño peppers, seeded and finely chopped ($1/4$ to $1/3$ cup)
$1/4$ cup snipped fresh cilantro
$1/4$ cup sugar

1. Combine tomatillos, apples, sweet pepper, vinegar, jalapeño peppers, cilantro, sugar, and 1 teaspoon *salt* in a 4- to 6-quart kettle. Bring to boiling.
2. Reduce heat and simmer, uncovered, 15 minutes. Ladle into hot, sterilized half-pint jars, leaving $1/2$-inch headspace. Adjust lids. Process in boiling-water canner for 10 minutes. Makes 5 half-pints, 5 gifts.

Lemon-Garlic Vinegar

1 quart white wine vinegar *or* distilled vinegar
Peel of 2 lemons
2 cloves garlic, crushed
Lemon peel (optional)

1. Heat vinegar in saucepan (do not boil). Place peel and garlic in crock or jar. Pour hot vinegar over. Cover; let stand in dark place 2 to 4 weeks.
2. Check vinegar for flavor. Strain into clean bottles. If desired, thread lemon peel on wooden skewer; insert in bottles. Makes 1 quart.

Friends will think of you when they enjoy Blueberry Sauce in the morning at breakfast or for an evening ice-cream treat.

Blueberry Sauce

 1   package (16 ounces) frozen blueberries, thawed
 1   cup water
 $^1/_2$ cup light corn syrup
 $^1/_4$ cup lemon juice
 1   package powdered fruit pectin
 $^1/_2$ teaspoon ground nutmeg
 $2^1/_2$ cups sugar

1. Combine the blueberries, water, corn syrup, lemon juice, pectin, and nutmeg in a
6- or 8-quart kettle. Bring mixture to a full rolling boil, stirring constantly. Stir in
sugar. Return to a full rolling boil. Boil hard for 1 minute, stirring constantly. Remove
from heat.
2. Ladle at once into hot, sterilized half-pint jars, leaving $^1/_4$-inch headspace. Adjust
lids. Process in boiling-water canner 15 minutes.
3. For giving, place a cloth or paper doily or circle of fabric over top of jar; tie with
ribbon. Include a card with this serving suggestion: *Serve warm over waffles or pancakes or
ice cream.* Makes 5 half-pints, 5 gifts.

Miniature Amaretto Cakes

1 cup butter
4 eggs
2 cups all-purpose flour
1½ teaspoons baking powder
¼ teaspoon ground nutmeg
1½ cups sugar
1 cup amaretto
1½ teaspoons finely shredded lemon peel
1 teaspoon vanilla
3 tablespoons brown sugar
3 tablespoons light corn syrup

1. Generously grease and flour eight 4-inch fluted tube pans or twenty 2½-inch muffin pans. Let butter and eggs stand at room temperature 30 minutes.
2. Stir together flour, baking powder, and nutmeg. In a large mixing bowl beat butter with electric mixer on medium speed for 30 seconds. Add *1 cup* of the sugar, 2 tablespoons at a time, beating on medium-high speed about 6 minutes or till mixture is very light and fluffy. Add eggs, one at a time, beating 1 minute after each addition, scraping bowl often. Stir in *⅓ cup* of the amaretto, the lemon peel and vanilla. Gradually add flour mixture, beating on medium-low speed just till combined.
3. Pour batter into prepared pans. Bake in a 325° oven 20 to 25 minutes for 4-inch pans, 22 minutes for muffin pans, or till a toothpick inserted near center comes out clean. Cool on rack 10 minutes. Remove cakes from pans. Cool thoroughly. Prick fluted top and sides of each cake or top and sides of each cupcake generously with tines of a fork.
4. For syrup, in saucepan combine remaining sugar, brown sugar, corn syrup, and ⅓ cup *water*. Cook and stir over medium heat till bubbly and sugar is dissolved; remove from heat. Stir in remaining amaretto. Cool 5 minutes.
5. Dip top and sides of each cake or top and sides of each cupcake into syrup. Place on wire rack above a baking sheet. Spoon or brush remaining syrup over tops of cakes. Cool. Wrap cakes individually in plastic wrap; chill up to 3 weeks. (Or, transfer to a tightly covered container and chill up to 3 weeks.)
6. For giving, place the individually wrapped cakes in a tissue-paper-lined box. Or place on foil-covered cardboard and overwrap with cellophane. Makes 8 miniature cakes or 20 cupcakes, 4 gifts.

Brandied Berry Sauce

3 cups cranberries
2 cups sugar
1 cup orange juice
⅛ teaspoon ground cloves
2 tablespoons cornstarch
2 tablespoons cold water
¼ cup brandy

1. Combine berries, sugar, orange juice, and cloves in small saucepan. Bring to boiling; reduce heat to medium. Simmer, uncovered, till berries pop.
2. Stir together cornstarch and water; stir into the cranberry mixture. Cook and stir till thickened and bubbly; cook and stir 2 minutes more. Stir in brandy.
3. Store in refrigerator or freeze in freezer containers. Makes 3½ cups.

*Rich butter cake is soaked
with amaretto syrup for these
little temptations. Miniature
Amaretto Cakes (recipe,
opposite) are great gifts.*

2 large oranges
2 large lemons
1 cup unsweetened pineapple juice
1 can (20 ounces) crushed pineapple (juice pack)
1 package (1³/4 ounces) powdered fruit pectin
5 cups sugar

Pineapple Marmalade

1. Score citrus peels into 4 lengthwise sections. Remove peels with a vegetable peeler.
Cut into very thin strips. In medium saucepan combine peels and pineapple juice. Bring
to boiling. Cover and simmer 20 minutes; do not drain.
2. Cut white membrane off fruit. Section fruit over bowl to catch juices. Discard seeds.
Add fruits and juices to peel mixture. Simmer, covered, 10 minutes more. Add
undrained pineapple.
3. Transfer fruit mixture to an 8-quart Dutch oven; stir in pectin. Bring to full rolling
boil, stirring constantly. Stir in sugar; return to full rolling boil. Boil hard 1 minute,
stirring constantly. Remove from heat; quickly skim off foam.
4. Ladle at once into hot, sterilized half-pint jars, leaving ¹/4-inch headspace. Wipe
rims; adjust lids. Process in boiling-water bath 15 minutes (start timing when water
boils). Makes 7 half-pints.

Recipe Index

Candies

Cookies

Desserts

Main Dishes

Recipe Index

continued